THE Blues BOOK

EASY GUITAR

2nd EDITION

ISBN 978-0-7935-9279-1

HAL•LEONARD®
CORPORATION

7777 W. BLUEMOUND RD. P.O. BOX 13819 MILWAUKEE, WI 53213

For all works contained herein:
Unauthorized copying, arranging, adapting, recording or public performance is an infringement of copyright.
Infringers are liable under the law.

Visit Hal Leonard Online at
www.halleonard.com

THE Blues BOOK

STRUM AND PICK PATTERNS

This chart contains the suggested strum and pick patterns that are referred to by number at the beginning of each song in this book. The symbols ⊓ and ∨ in the strum patterns refer to down and up strokes, respectively. The letters in the pick patterns indicate which right-hand fingers plays which strings.

p = thumb
i = index finger
m = middle finger
a = ring finger

For example; Pick Pattern 2
is played: thumb - index - middle - ring

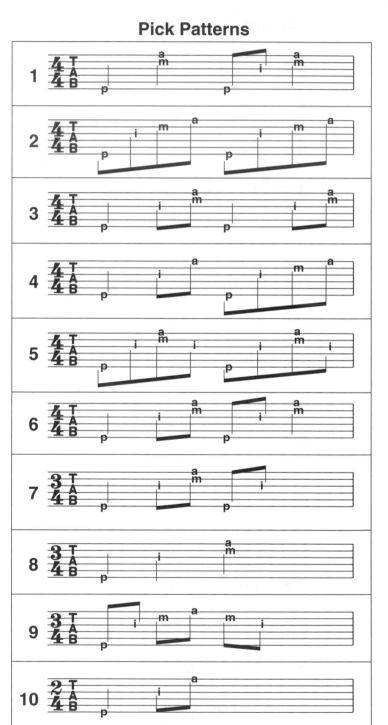

Strum Patterns

Pick Patterns

You can use the 3/4 Strum or Pick Patterns in songs written in compound meter (6/8, 9/8, 12/8, etc.).
For example, you can accompany a song in 6/8 by playing the 3/4 pattern twice in each measure.
The 4/4 Strum and Pick Patterns can be used for songs written in cut time (¢) by doubling the note time values in the patterns. Each pattern would therefore last two measures in cut time.

As the Years Go Passing By

Words and Music by Deadric Malone

Strum Pattern: 2, 4
Pick Pattern: 2, 4

Verse

Slow Blues

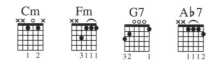

1. There is noth-in' I can do, ____ as you leave me ____ here to
2., 3., 4. *See Additional Lyrics*

cry. ____ There is noth-ing I can do, ____

as you leave me here to cry. ____ You know my

love ____ will fol-low you, ___ as the years go pass-in' by. _____

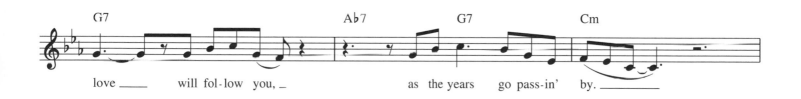

1., 2., 3. **4.**

2. Give you

Additional Lyrics

2. Give you all that I own, that's one thing you can't deny.
   Give you all that I own, that's one thing you can't deny.
   You know my love will follow you as the years go passin' by.

3., 4. Gonna leave it up to you, so long, so long, goodbye.
   You know my love will follow you,
   As the years go passin' by.

Copyright © 1959 SONGS OF UNIVERSAL, INC.
Copyright Renewed
All Rights Reserved   Used by Permission

Baby Please Don't Go

Words and Music by Joseph Lee Williams

Strum Pattern: 3, 5
Pick Pattern: 3, 5

Chorus
Moderate Blues

Oh, ba - by, please don't go. ____

Oh, ba - by, please don't go. ____

Oh, ba - by, please _ don't _ go back to New Or - leans _ be - cause I

love ____ you so. ____

Verse

1. Oh, turn your lamp down low. ____
2. *See Additional Lyrics*

Oh, turn your lamp down low. ____

Oh, turn your lamp _ down _ low, be - cause I love you so. ____ Ba - by,

© 1944 (Renewed 1972) EMI FULL KEEL MUSIC
All Rights Reserved   International Copyright Secured   Used by Permission

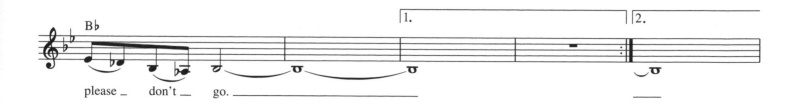

please __ don't __ go. ____

Chorus

Oh, ba - by, please don't go. ____

____ Oh, ba - by, please don't go!

Additional Lyrics

2. They got me 'way down here,
   They got me 'way down here.
   They got me 'way down here by the rollin' fog,
   Treat me like a dog.

Baby What's Wrong

Words and Music by Jimmy Reed

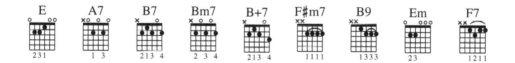

Strum Pattern: 2, 4
Pick Pattern: 2, 3

Verse
Moderately

1. Hey, (3.) ba - by, hon - ey what's wrong with

you? ____ Hey,

ba - by, hon - ey what's wrong with

Copyright © 1961 (Renewed) by Conrad Music, a division of Arc Music Corp. (BMI) and Seeds of Reed Music (BMI)
International Copyright Secured   All Rights Reserved
Used by Permission

you? _____ You

don't treat me, dar - lin', like you used to

do. _____ 2., 4. You

Verse

got me run - nin' ba - by, you got me hid - in', too,

tell me, tell me ba - by, what we gon - na do, hey,

ba - by, hon - ey what's wrong with

you? _____ You

don't treat me, dar - lin', like you used to

do. _____ 3. Hey,

8

Before You Accuse Me
(Take a Look at Yourself)

Words and Music by Ellas McDaniels

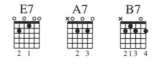

Strum Pattern: 1
Pick Pattern: 2

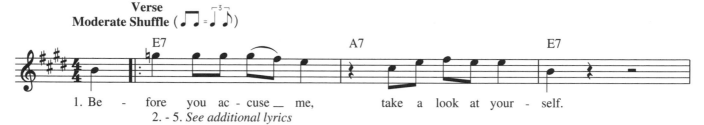

1. Be - fore you ac - cuse __ me, take a look at your - self.
2. - 5. *See additional lyrics*

Be - fore you ac - cuse __ me, take a look at your - self.

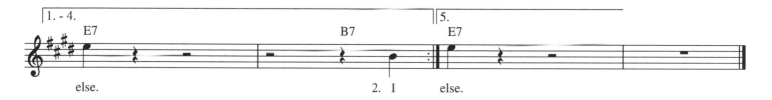

You said I'm spend - in' my mon - ey on oth - er wom - en, you're ta - kin' mon - ey from some - one

else.　　　　　　2. I　else.

Additional Lyrics

2. I called your mama 'bout three or four nights ago.
   I called your mama 'bout three or four nights ago.
   Well, your mama said "Son don't call my daughter no more."

3. Before you 'cuse me, take a look at yourself.
   Before you 'cuse me, take a look at yourself.
   You say I'm spendin' my money on other women,
   You takin' money from someone else.

4. Come on back home, baby, try my love one more time.
   Come on back home, baby, try my love one more time.
   You know if things don't go to suit you, I think I'll lose my mind.

5. Before you 'cuse me, take a look at yourself.
   Before you 'cuse me, take a look at yourself.
   You say I'm spendin' my money on other women,
   You takin' money from someone else.

© 1957 (Renewed 1985) EMI LONGITUDE MUSIC
All Rights Reserved   International Copyright Secured   Used by Permission

Blues Before Sunrise

Words and Music by Leroy Carr

Strum Pattern: 4
Pick Pattern: 1

Verse
Moderate Blues

1. I had the blues be-fore sun-rise, with tears stand-ing in _ my eyes. _____
2., 3., 4. *See Additional Lyrics*

I had the blues be-fore sun-rise, with tears stand-ing in _ my eyes. _____

It's such a mis-'ra-ble feel-ing, a feel-in' that I feel de-spised. _____

Verse

_____ 5. Now, I love my ba-by, but my ba-by won't _ be-have. _____

Now, I love my ba-by, _____ but my ba-by won't be-have, _

I'm gon-na buy me a sharp-shoot-in' pis-tol, _ and put her in her grave. _____

Additional Lyrics

2. Seems like ev'rybody, ev'rybody's down on me.
   Seems like ev'rybody, ev'rybody's down on me.
   I'm gonna cast my troubles, down in the deep blue sea.

3. Today has been such a long, long, lonesome day.
   Today has been a long, long, lonesome day.
   I've been sittin' here thinkin' with my mind a million miles away.

4. Blues start to roll in, and stop at my front door.
   Blues start to roll in, and stop at my front door.
   I'm gonna change my way of living, ain't gonna worry no more.

Copyright © 1950 UNIVERSAL MUSIC CORP.
Copyright Renewed
All Rights Reserved   Used by Permission

The Blues Is Alright

Words and Music by Milton Campbell

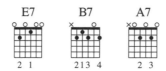

Strum Pattern: 3
Pick Pattern: 3

Intro

Fast Blues

1. I got this song I'm gon-na sing. _ I'm gon-na sing it just for

2., 3., 4. *See additional lyrics*

you. If you dig the blues, I want you to help me sing it, too.

I want ev-'ry-bod-y hear me when I say, _ that the blues _ is back and it's

here to stay. Let me ex-plain it to you. 2. I used to why I can say this to-night.

Chorus

Hey, hey, _ the blues is al-right. Hey, hey, _ the blues is al-right.

Hey, hey, _ the blues is al-right. Hey, hey, _ the

Copyright © 1982 by Peermusic III, Ltd., Malaco Music and Trice Publishing Company
International Copyright Secured   All Rights Reserved

blues is al - right. It's al - right, (Al - right.) it's al - right, (Al - right.) ev - 'ry - day and

night.   4. I'm

Additional Lyrics

2. I used to have someone that meant the whole world to me.
   But she left me for someone else, left my heart in misery.
   That's when I found out the blues would always be a part of me.
   Let me tell you this.

3. You see when she left me, she gave me the blues.
   That was the last thing I thought I could use.
   But now I'm glad she left me, I'm glad she gave me the blues.
   You see I went out and found me, I went out and found me someone new.
   That's why I can say this tonight.

4. I'm glad she left me, I'm glad she gave me the blues.
   You see I'm grateful to the blues, it was the blues that brought me to you.
   You see if she'd never given me the blues, I never would have found someone sweet like you.
   That's why I can say, y'all.

Cold Shot

Words and Music by Mike Kindred and Wesley Clark

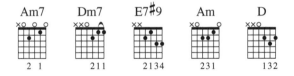

Strum Pattern: 3
Pick Pattern: 3

Intro
Moderate Shuffle

Verse

1. Once was a sweet thing, ba - by,   we held our love in our   hands.   But
2. *See additional lyrics*

Copyright © 1984 Hard Case Music
All Rights Administered by Chrysalis Songs
All Rights Reserved   Used by Permission

now __ I reach __ to kiss your __ lips, __ my touch don't mean a thing. __ And that's a cold shot, __

% Chorus

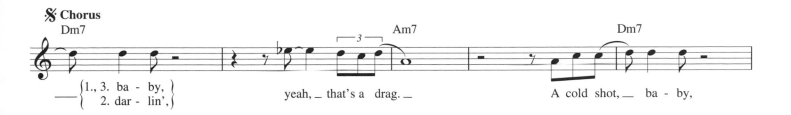

{1., 3. ba - by,}
{2. dar - lin',}   yeah, __ that's a drag. __   A cold shot, __ ba - by,

To Coda ⊕ | 1.
Interlude

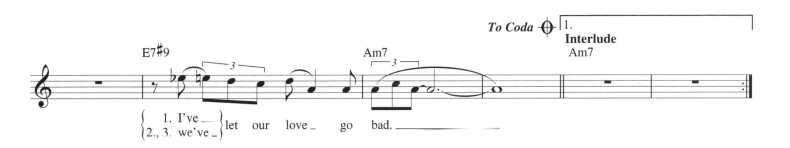

{ 1. I've __ }
{2., 3. we've __} let our love __ go bad. __

| 2.
Verse

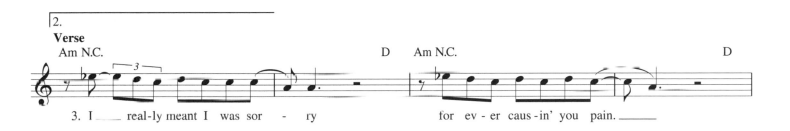

3. I __ real-ly meant I was sor - ry   for ev - er caus-in' you pain. __

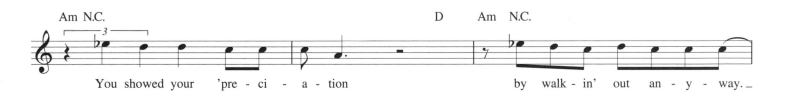

You showed your 'pre - ci - a - tion   by walk - in' out an - y - way. __

⊕ **Coda**

D.S. al Coda   **Outro**   *Repeat and fade*

__ And that's a cold shot, __

Additional Lyrics

2. Remember the way that you loved me,
   You'd do anything I said.
   And now I see you out somewhere,
   You won't give me the time of day.

Blues with a Feeling

Words and Music by Walter Jacobs

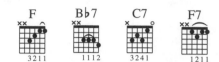

Strum Pattern: 4, 6
Pick Pattern: 3, 5

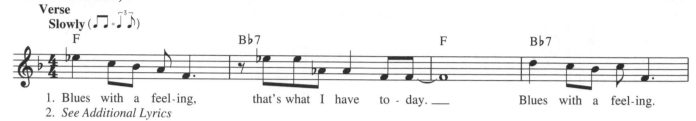

1. Blues with a feel-ing, that's what I have to-day. ___ Blues with a feel-ing.
2. *See Additional Lyrics*

that's what I have to - day; ___ I'm gon - na find my ba - by,

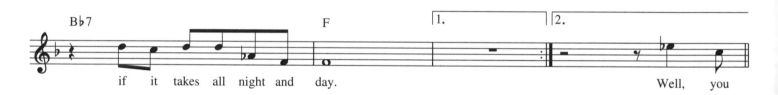

if it takes all night and day. Well, you

know I love you, ba - by, I won - der the rea - son why. You told me you loved me, ba - by, and you

left me here to cry. ___ Blues with a feel-ing, that's what I have to - day. ___

I'm gon - na find my ba - by, if it takes all night and day.

Additional Lyrics

2. What a lonesome feeling, when you're by yourself.
What a lonesome feeling, when you're by yourself.
When the one that you're lovin' has gone away and left.

Copyright © 1963 (Renewed) by Arc Music Corporation (BMI)
International Copyright Secured   All Rights Reserved
Used by Permission

Boogie Chillen No. 2

Words and Music by John Lee Hooker and Bernard Besman

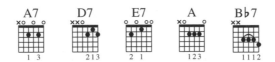

Strum Pattern: 3, 5
Pick Pattern: 3, 5

Verse
Moderate Blues

1. I'm goin' a-way, babe, but I will be com-ing back. _____ I'm

goin' a-way, babe, ____ but I will be ____ com-ing back. I'm a

man now, ba-by, and ___ I sure ___ can have my fun. _____ 2. My

Verse

ba-by got some-thin' round like an ap-ple, shaped like a pear. Sure ___ now, babe. My ba-

- by got some-thin'. My ba-by got some-thin'. My ba-

- by got some-thin', man, ___ I sure do love. _____

Copyright © 1970 by Universal Music - Careers and Sony/ATV Music Publishing LLC
Copyright Renewed
All Rights on behalf of Sony/ATV Songs LLC Administered by Sony/ATV Music Publishing LLC, 8 Music Square West, Nashville, TN 37203
International Copyright Secured   All Rights Reserved

Born Under a Bad Sign

Words and Music by Booker T. Jones and William Bell

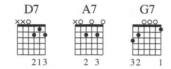

Strum Pattern: 1
Pick Pattern: 2

Chorus
Moderately

Born un-der a bad sign. Been down _ since I be-gan to crawl. _

If it was-n't for bad luck, you know I would-n't have no luck at all.

Verse

1. Hard luck and trou-ble been my on-ly friend. I been on my own
2., 3. *See additional lyrics*

ev-er since I ___ was ten. to my grave. ___

Additional Lyrics

2. I can't read, I didn't learn how to write.
   My whole life has been one big fight.

3. You know wine and women is all I crave.
   A big leg woman gonna carry me to my grave.

Copyright © 1967 IRVING MUSIC, INC.
Copyright Renewed
All Rights Reserved   Used by Permission

Come On in My Kitchen

Words and Music by Robert Johnson

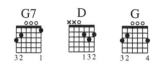

Strum Pattern: 3, 6
Pick Pattern: 3, 5

Verse
Moderately

1. The wom-an I love, took from my best friend. _____ Some jok - er got
2.-5. *See Additional Lyrics*

luck - y, stole her back a - gain. You bet-ter come on in my kitch -

en, babe, it's goin' to be rain - in' out-doors. __

1. - 4.   5.

Additional Lyrics

2. Oh, she's gone, I know she won't come back.
   I've taken the last nickel out of her ration sack.
   You better come on in my kitchen, baby, it's goin' to be rainin' outdoors.

3. *Spoken: Oh, can't you hear the wind howl?*
   Can't you hear that wind howl?
   You better come on in my kitchen, baby, it's goin' to be rainin' outdoors.

4. When a woman gets in trouble, everybody throws her down.
   Lookin' for her good friend, none can't be found.
   You better come on in my kitchen, baby, it's goin' to be rainin' outdoors.

5. Winter time's comin', it's goin' to be slow.
   You can make the winter, babe, that's dry long so.
   You better come on in my kitchen, 'cause it's goin' to be rainin' outdoors.

Copyright © (1978), 1990, 1991 MPCA King Of Spades (SESAC) and Claud L. Johnson
Administered by Music & Media International, Inc.
International Copyright Secured   All Rights Reserved

Confessin' the Blues

Words and Music by Walter Brown and Jay McShann

Strum Pattern: 2, 4
Pick Pattern: 2, 4

Intro
Moderate Blues

1. Ba - by,

%‐ **Verse**

here I stand be-fore you with my heart in my hand. I want you to read it {ma - ma / pa - pa} hop - in'
2., 3., 4. *See Additional Lyrics*

that you'll un - der-stand. Well, _____ babe, _____ {ma - ma / pa - pa} please _ don't dog me

'round. _____ I'd rath - er love you, ba - by,

1.

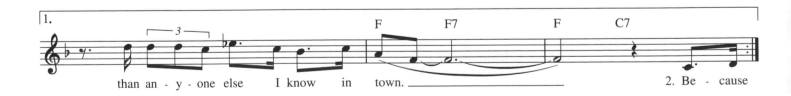

than an - y - one else I know in town. _____ 2. Be - cause

Copyright © 1941 Sony/ATV Music Publishing LLC and Universal Music Corp.
Copyright Renewed
All Rights on behalf of Sony/ATV Tunes LLC Administered by Sony/ATV Music Publishing LLC, 8 Music Square West, Nashville, TN 37203
International Copyright Secured   All Rights Reserved

well, I swear ___ I hope to die. _____ Well,

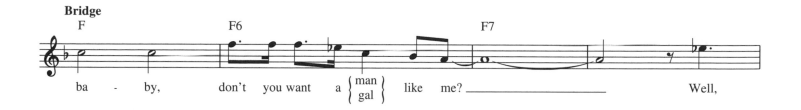

Bridge

ba - by, don't you want a { man / gal } like me? _____ Well,

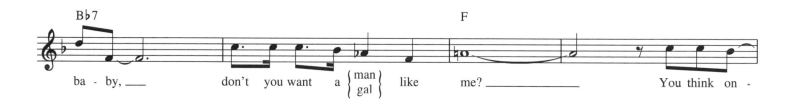

ba - by, ___ don't you want a { man / gal } like me? _____ You think on -

- ly of our fu - ture, for - get a - bout your used ___ to be. _____

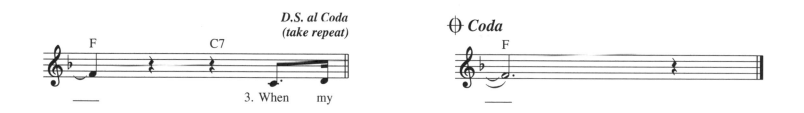

D.S. al Coda
(take repeat)

___ 3. When my

⊕ Coda

___

Additional Lyrics

2. Because you're so nice and lovin' and you have such pleasin' ways,
   If you take me to your home be there, be there all my days.
   That's the truth, { mama. / papa. } Well, you know I wasn't lyin'.
   If I don't love you, babe, well, I swear I hope to die.

3. When my days are long and dreary and the sun refuses to shine,
   I would never be blue and lonely if I knew that you were mine.
   Well, babe, will you make ev'rything all right?
   Can I meet you today, babe,
   Or will it be tomorrow night?

4. This is my confession { mama / papa } and I'm thrilled by all your charms.
   Well, it seems that I'm in heaven when you hold me in your arms.
   Well, babe, you can have me for yourself.
   You are meant for me, { mama. / papa. }
   I don't want nobody else.

Crosscut Saw

Words and Music by R.G. Ford

Strum Pattern: 2
Pick Pattern: 3

Chorus
Moderately

I'm a cross-cut saw, __ ba-by, just drag __ me a-cross __ your log.

You know I'm a cross-cut saw, __ just drag me a-cross your log. __

I'll cut your wood so eas-y for you, you can't help but say, __ "Hot dog."

Verse

1. Now, some call me wood-chop-pin' Sam, some call me wood-cut-tin' Jim. __ The
2. *See additional lyrics*

last girl I cut the wood for, you know, she want me __ back a-gain. I'm a cross-cut saw, __

just drag me a-cross your log. __ I'll cut your wood so eas-y for you,

you can't help but say, __ "Hot dog." 2. I

Additional Lyrics

2. I got a double-bladed axe that really cuts good.
   But I'm a crosscut saw, just bury me in your wood.
   I'm a crosscut saw, baby, just drag me across your log.
   I'll cut your wood so easy for you, woman,
   You can't but say, "Hot dog."

Copyright © 1969 IRVING MUSIC, INC.
Copyright Renewed
All Rights Reserved   Used by Permission

Cross Road Blues
(Crossroads)

Words and Music by Robert Johnson

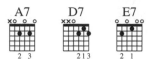

Strum Pattern: 1
Pick Pattern: 2

Intro
Fast Blues

to the cross - road, fell down on my knee. ___
2. - 4. *See Additional Lyrics*

Down ___ to the cross - road, fell down on my knee. ___

Asked the Lord a - bove for mer - cy,

"Take me if you please." ___   2. I went down ___

down.   *Additional Lyrics*

Additional Lyrics

2. I went down to the crossroad, tried to flag a ride.
   Down to the crossroad, tried to flag a ride.
   Nobody seemed to know me. Ev'rybody passed me by.

3. When I'm goin' down to Rosedale, take my rider by my side.
   Goin' down to Rosedale, take my rider by my side.
   We can still barrelhouse, baby, on the riverside.

4. You can run, you can run. Tell my friend, boy, Willie Brown.
   Run, you can run. Tell my friend, boy, Willie Brown.
   And I'm standin' at the crossroad. Believe I'm sinkin' down.

Copyright © (1978), 1990, 1991 MCPA King Of Spades (SESAC) and Claud L. Johnson
Administered by Music & Media International, Inc.
International Copyright Secured   All Rights Reserved

Damn Right, I've Got the Blues

By Buddy Guy

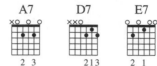

Strum Pattern: 5
Pick Pattern: 1

Intro
Slow Shuffle

1. You're (3.) damn right, I've got the blues from my head down to my
2. *See additional lyrics*

shoes.   You're damn right, I got the blues

from my head down to my shoes.   I can't win

'cause I don't have a thing to lose.   3. You're

You damn right, I've got the blues.

Additional Lyrics

2. I stopped by my daughter's house. You know I just want to use the phone.
I stopped by my daughter's house. You know I just want to use the phone.
You know, my little grandbaby came to the door and say,
"Granddaddy, you know ain't no one at home."

Copyright © 1991 by Mic-Shau Music Company
All Rights Administered by Universal Music - Z Songs
International Copyright Secured   All Rights Reserved

Do You Know What It Means to Miss New Orleans

Written by Eddie De Lange and Louis Alter

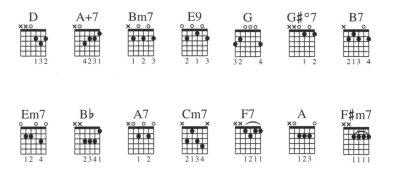

Strum Pattern: 1, 3
Pick Pattern: 1, 3

Verse
Slowly

1. Do you know what it means _ to miss New Or - leans _ and miss it each night _ and

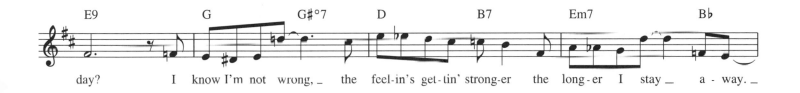

day? I know I'm not wrong, _ the feel-in's get-tin' strong-er the long-er I stay _ a - way. _

Verse

_ 2. Miss the moss-cov-ered vines, _ the tall sug - ar pines _ where mock-in'-birds used _ to

sing and I'd like to see _ the la - zy Mis-sis-sip-pi a - hur-ry-in' in - to spring. _

Bridge

_ The moon - light on the bay - ou _ a Cre-ole tune _ that fills the air; I

© 1946 (Renewed 1974, 2002) DE LANGE MUSIC CO. (ASCAP)/Administered by
BUG MUSIC and LOUIS ALTER MUSIC PUBLICATIONS, New York
All Rights outside the United States Controlled by EDWIN H. MORRIS & COMPANY, A Division of MPL MUSIC PUBLISHING, INC.
All Rights Reserved   Used by Permission

Double Trouble

Words and Music by Otis Rush

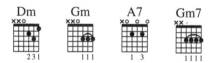

Strum Pattern: 1, 3
Pick Pattern: 1, 3

Verse
Slow Blues

Copyright © 1965, 1968 (Renewed) by Conrad Music, a division of Arc Music Corp. (BMI)
International Copyright Secured   All Rights Reserved
Used by Permission

they say you can make it ___ if you try. _____ Yes, in this gen-er-a-tion of _ mil-lion-aires, it's

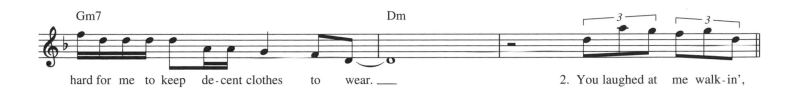

hard for me to keep de-cent clothes to wear. ___ 2. You laughed at me walk-in',

Verse

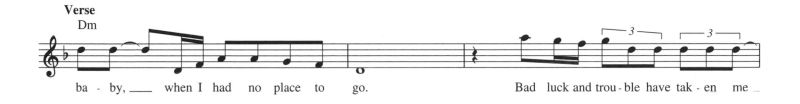

ba - by, ___ when I had no place to go. Bad luck and trou-ble have tak-en me

___ I have got no mon-ey to show. ___ Hey, hey, to make it you've got to try,

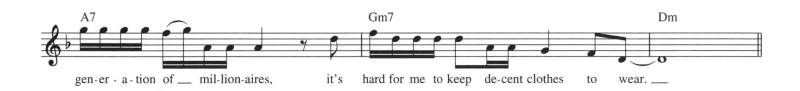

ba - by ___ that's no lie. _____ Yes, in this

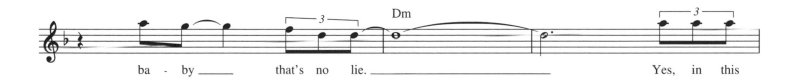

gen-er-a-tion of ___ mil-lion-aires, it's hard for me to keep de-cent clothes to wear. ___

Outro

Drunken Hearted Man

Words and Music by Robert Johnson

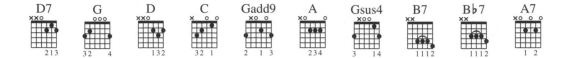

Strum Pattern: 2, 4
Pick Pattern: 2, 4

Verse
Moderately

1. I'm the drunk-en heart - ed man. My life seems so mis-er - y.
2., 3., 4. *See Additional Lyrics*

I'm the poor drunk - en heart - ed man. My life seems so mis-er - y.

And if I could on - ly change my way of liv - in', it would

mean so much to me. 2. I been dogged

Additional Lyrics

2. I been dogged and I been driven eve' since I left my mother's home.
   I been dogged and I been driven eve' since I left my mother's home.
   And I can't see the reason why
   That I can't leave these no good womens alone.

3. My poor father died and left me and my mother done the best she could.
   My poor father died and left me and my mother done the best she could.
   Every man love that game you call love
   But it don't mean no man no good.

4. I'm the poor drunken hearted man and sin was the cause of it all.
   I'm a poor drunken hearted man and sin was the cause of it all.
   But the day you get weak for no good women,
   That's the day that you surely fall.

Copyright © (1978), 1990, 1991 MPCA King Of Spades (SESAC) and Claud L. Johnson
Administered by Music & Media International, Inc.
International Copyright Secured   All Rights Reserved

Everyday I Have the Blues

Words and Music by Peter Chatman

Strum Pattern: 4, 6
Pick Pattern: 3, 5

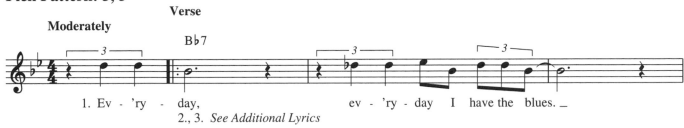

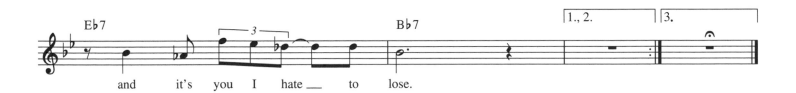

Additional Lyrics

2. Nobody loves me, nobody seems to care.
   Nobody loves me, nobody seems to care.
   Speakin' of worries and troubles, darlin',
   You know I've had my share.

3. Every day, every day, every day, every day,
   Every day, every day I have the blues.
   When you see me worryin', woman,
   Honey, it's you I hate to lose.

Copyright © 1952 (Renewed) by Arc Music Corporation (BMI), Fort Knox Music Inc. and Trio Music Company
International Copyright Secured   All Rights Reserved
Used by Permission

Fine and Mellow

Words and Music by Billie Holiday

Copyright © 1940 by Edward B. Marks Music Company
Copyright Renewed
International Copyright Secured   All Rights Reserved
Reprinted by Permission

make you drink and gam-ble, make you stay out all night long. ____

Love will make you do things that you know is wrong. ____ 4. But if you

Verse

treat me right ba - by, I'll stay home ev-'ry day; ____ if you

treat me right ba - by, I'll stay home ev-'ry day. ____ But you're so

mean to me ba - by, I know you're gon-na drive me a-way. 5. Love is

Verse

just like a fau - cet, it turns off and on. ____

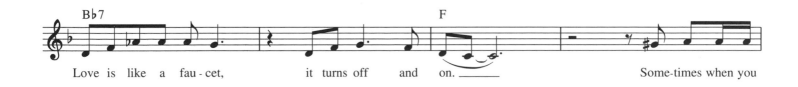
Love is like a fau - cet, it turns off and on. ____ Some-times when you

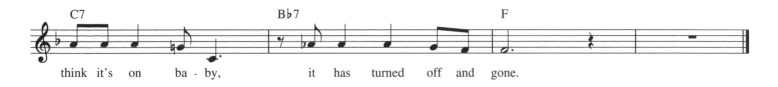
think it's on ba - by, it has turned off and gone.

Five Long Years

Words and Music by Eddie Boyd

Strum Pattern: 8
Pick Pattern: 8

Verse

Moderately

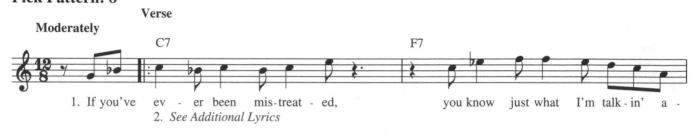

1. If you've ev - er been mis-treat - ed, you know just what I'm talk - in' a -
2. *See Additional Lyrics*

bout. If you've ev - er been mis-treat - ed,

you know just what I talk - in' a - bout. I work

five long years for one wom - an, and she had the nerve

to kick me out. 2. I got a out.

Additional Lyrics

2. I got a job at a steel mill, truckin' steel just like a slave.
Five long years of fright I'm runnin', straight home with all of my pay.
Mistreated, you know what I'm talkin' about?
I work five long years for one woman, and she had the nerve to throw me out.

Copyright © 1952 (Renewed) by Embassy Music Corporation (BMI)
International Copyright Secured   All Rights Reserved
Reprinted by Permission

Further On Up the Road

Words and Music by Joe Veasey and Don Robey

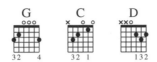

Strum Pattern: 3
Pick Pattern: 3

Verse
Moderate Shuffle

1., 3. Fur-ther on up the road some-one's gon-na hurt you like you hurt me.
2. *See Additional Lyrics*

Fur-ther on up the road ___ some-one's gon-na hurt you like you hurt me.

play 3 times

Fur-ther on up the road, ba - by, you just wait and see.

Outro

You been laugh-in' pret-ty ba - by; Some - day you're gon-na be cry - in'.

You been laugh-in' pret-ty ba - by; Some - day you're gon-na be cry - in'.

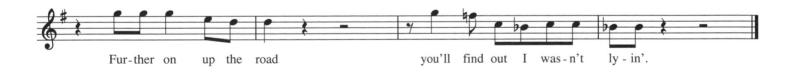

Fur-ther on up the road you'll find out I was-n't ly - in'.

Additional Lyrics

2. You got to reap just what you sow,
   That old saying is true.
   You got to reap just what you sow,
   That old saying is true.
   Just like you mistreat someone,
   Someone's gonna mistreat you.

Copyright © 1957 SONGS OF UNIVERSAL, INC.
Copyright Renewed
All Rights Reserved   Used by Permission

Gambler's Blues

Words and Music by B.B. King and Johnny Pate

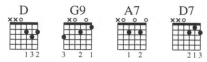

Copyright © 1967 SONGS OF UNIVERSAL, INC., YVONNE PUBLISHING CO. and UNIVERSAL MUSIC - CAREERS
Copyright Renewed
All Rights Controlled and Administered by SONGS OF UNIVERSAL, INC.
All Rights Reserved   Used by Permission

much a-bout the dice. ___ Oh, ___ but I'll wa-ger my ba-by knows,

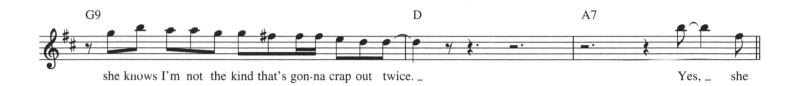

she knows I'm not the kind that's gon-na crap out twice. ___ Yes, ___ she

Outro

left me ear-ly this morn - ing. I don't know the rea-son why. ___ She just

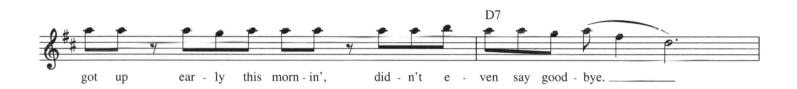

got up ear-ly this morn-in', did-n't e-ven say good-bye. _____

But I love you, I love you, you know I love you, ba - by, al -

- though you've made __ me cry. ___ Yes, there are a lot of wom-en who want me,

oh, ___ but how ___ you sat - is - fy! _____

Additional Lyrics

2. They say love is just a proposition, people;
   It's strictly a game of give and take.
   Yeah, they tell me love, love, love is a proposition, people;
   They tell you it's strictly a game of give and take.
   Woah, but my woman took all I gave her,
   And I'm here to tell you that love proposition stuff's a fake!

Gee Baby, Ain't I Good to You

Words by Don Redman and Andy Razaf
Music by Don Redman

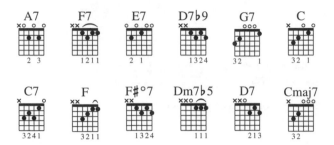

Strum Pattern: 4
Pick Pattern: 1

Verse
Slow Blues

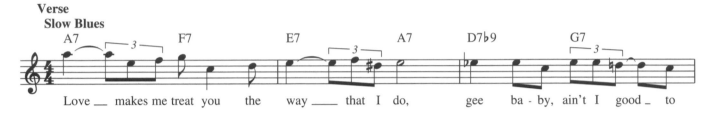

Love __ makes me treat you the way __ that I do, gee ba - by, ain't I good __ to

you! There's noth - in' too good for a girl __ that's so true, gee ba - by, ain't I good __ to

you! Brought you a fur coat for Christ - mas, a dia-mond ring, __

a Cad - il - lac car, an' ev - 'ry - thing. __ Love __ makes me treat you the

way __ that I do, gee ba - by, ain't I good __ to you. you.

© 1929 CAPITOL SONGS, INC. and MICHAEL H. GOLDSEN, INC.
© Renewed 1957, 1985 MICHAEL H. GOLDSEN, INC. and EDWIN H. MORRIS & COMPANY, A Division of MPL Music Publishing, Inc.
All Rights Reserved

Got to Hurry

By Oscar Rasputin

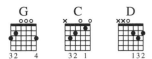

Strum Pattern: 1
Pick Pattern: 2

Gtr. ad lib. on repeats

Repeat and Fade

© 1965 (Renewed 1993) GLENWOOD MUSIC CORP. and EMI MUSIC PUBLISHING LTD.
All Rights Controlled and Administered by COLGEMS-EMI MUSIC INC.
All Rights Reserved   International Copyright Secured   Used by Permission

Good Morning Little Schoolgirl

Words and Music by Sonny Boy Williamson

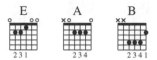

Strum Pattern: 1, 6
Pick Pattern: 1, 3

Intro
Bright Rock

Oh, oh, oh, oh, oh.

Oh, oh, oh, oh, oh.   Oh, oh, oh, oh, oh.

Oh, oh, oh, oh, oh.   Oh, oh, oh.   Oh, oh, oh, oh, oh.

% Verse

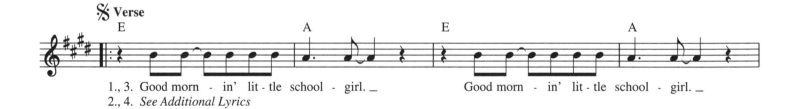

1., 3. Good morn - in' lit - tle school - girl. _   Good morn - in' lit - tle school - girl. _
2., 4. *See Additional Lyrics*

Can I ___ go ___ home with, _ a-won't you let me go ___ home with you, _ so I can

To Coda ⊕

hug, hug,   squeeze, squeeze.   If you let me, I can tease you ba — by.

Copyright © 1964 (Renewed) by Arc Music Corporation (BMI)
International Copyright Secured   All Rights Reserved
Used by Permission

Chorus

Hey, hey, hey, hey, hey, hey, h-hey, hey.

Hey, yeah.

Guitar Solo

D.S. al Coda
(take repeat)

✛ *Coda*
Outro

Repeat and Fade

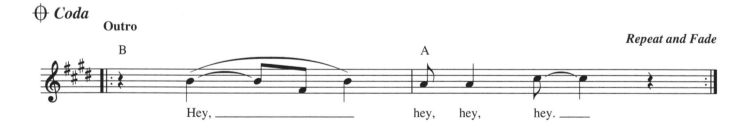

Hey, hey, hey, hey.

Additional Lyrics

Let's dance, little schoolgirl.
Let's dance, little schoolgirl.
Won't you let me take you to the hop, hop;
Have a party at the soda shop,
So we can do the twist, do the stroll,
To the music of the rock and roll, oh.

Good mornin' little schoolgirl.
Good mornin' little schoolgirl.
Can I go home with,
A-won't you let me go home with you?
Tell your mama and your papa that I love you.
Tell your sisters and your brother that I love you.

Have You Ever Loved a Woman

Words and Music by Billy Myles

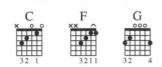

Strum Pattern: 8
Pick Pattern: 8
   Verse
      Moderate Blues

1. Have you ev-er loved _ a wom-an
2., 3. *See additional lyrics*

so _ much   you trem-ble in pain? _

Have you ev-er loved _ a wom-an

so much   you trem-ble in pain?

And all the

time, you know _____   she

bears _____ an-oth-er man's name. _____

Additional Lyrics

2. But you just love that woman so much, it's a shame and a sin.
   You just love that woman so much, it's a shame and a sin.
   But all the time, you know she belongs to your very best friend.

3. Have you ever loved a woman, oh, you know you can't leave her alone?
   Have you ever loved a woman, yes, you know you can't leave her alone?
   Something deep inside of you won't let you wreck your best friend's home.

Copyright © 1960 by Fort Knox Music Inc. and Trio Music Company
Copyright Renewed
International Copyright Secured   All Rights Reserved
Used by Permission

Honest I Do

Words and Music by Jimmy Reed and Ewart G. Abner, Jr.

Strum Pattern: 4, 5
Pick Pattern: 2, 3

Verse
Slowly

Don't you know that I love ___ you, hon-est I do. ___

I nev - er ___ placed ___ no one ___ a-bove you.

Please tell me you love ___ me, stop driv - ing me mad. ___

You're the sweet-est ___ lit-tle wom-an that I ev - er had.

Please tell me you love ___ me, ___ stop driv - ing me mad. ___

When I woke_ up this morn-ing nev-er felt ___ so bad.

Copyright © 1957 (Renewed) by Conrad Music, a division of Arc Music Corp. (BMI) and Seeds of Reed Music (BMI)
International Copyright Secured   All Rights Reserved
Used by Permission

Help Me

Words and Music by Sonny Boy Williamson, Ralph Bass and Willie Dixon

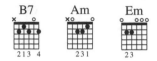

Strum Pattern: 3
Pick Pattern: 4

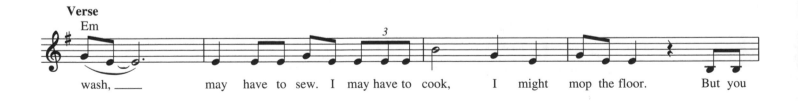

Copyright © 1963, 1970 (Renewed) by Arc Music Corporation (BMI)
International Copyright Secured   All Rights Reserved
Used by Permission

help me, dar - ling, —   I'll find my - self some - bod - y else.   3. When I

Verse

walk, _____ you walk with me.   And when I talk,   you talk to me.   Oh,

babe,   I can't do it all by my - self.   If you don't

help me dar - ling, —   I'll have to find some-bod - y else.   4. Bring my night

Verse

shirt.   Put on your morn - ing gown. _____   Oh,

bring me my night-shirt.   Put on your morn - ing gown.   Do not know

where she been   but I feel like ly - in' down.

Honey Bee

Written by McKinley Morganfield (Muddy Waters)

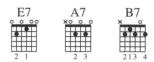

Strum Pattern: 8
Pick Pattern: 8

Verse

Moderately

1. Sail on,   sail on, my lit-tle hon-ey bee, sail on.

Sail on,   sail __ on my lit-tle hon-ey bee, sail __ on.

You gon-na keep on sail-in'   till you lose ____ your hap-py home.

Verse

2. Sail on,   sail on, my lit-tle hon-ey bee, sail on.

Sail on, _____   sail __ on, my lit-tle hon-ey bee, sail on.

I don't mind you sail-in', _   but please __ don't sail so long.   All right, lit-tle hon-ey bee.

© 1959 (Renewed 1987) WATERTOONS MUSIC (BMI)/Administered by BUG MUSIC
All Rights Reserved   Used by Permission

3. I hear a lot of buz-zing. _ Sounds _ like my lit-tle hon-ey bee. _

I hear a lot of buz-zing. _ Sounds _ like my lit-tle hon-ey bee.

She been all a-round the world mak-in' hon-ey, but now she is com-in' back _ home _ to me.

Matchbox

Words and Music by Carl Lee Perkins

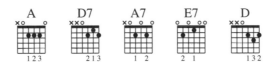

Strum Pattern: 1, 3
Pick Pattern: 1, 3

 **Verse**

Moderate Rock

1. Well, I'm (5.) sit-tin' here won-d'rin' would a match - box hold my clothes? Yeah, I'm
3. *See Additional Lyrics*

sit-tin' here won-d'rin' would a match - box hold my clothes? _ I ain't _

© 1957 KNOX MUSIC, INC.

© Renewed 1985 CARL PERKINS MUSIC, INC. (Administered by WREN MUSIC CO., A Division of MPL Music Publishing, Inc.)
All Rights Reserved

43

How Long, How Long Blues

Words and Music by Leroy Carr

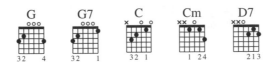

Strum Pattern: 1
Pick Pattern: 3

Verse
Slow Blues

How long, __ how long __ has that eve-nin' train been gone? How long, __

__ how long, __ ba-by how long? _____ Heard the whis-tle

blow-in', could-n't see __ no train. Way down in my __ heart I had an ach-in'

pain. How long, __ how long, __ ba-by how long? _____ I'm sad and

lone-ly all the whole_ day through. Why don't you write me and give me the

news? You have left me, __ left me sing-in' those how_ long blues. _____

Copyright © 1929, 1941 UNIVERSAL MUSIC CORP.
Copyright Renewed
All Rights Reserved Used by Permission

I'm Tore Down

Words and Music by Sonny Thompson

Strum Pattern: 3, 4
Pick Pattern: 3, 4

Chorus
Moderate Blues

I'm tore down. I'm al - most lev - el with the ground. _ I'm

tore down. _ I'm al - most lev - el with the ground. _ Why'd I

feel __ like this __ when my ba - by can't be found? __

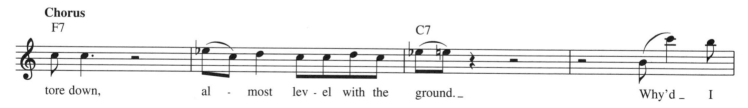

1. Went to the riv-er, to jump in. My ba - by showed up and said, "I will tell you when." Well, I'm

tore down, al - most lev - el with the ground. _ Why'd _ I

feel __ like this __ when my ba - by can't be found? __ 2. I

love you babe _ with all my heart and soul. _ Love like mine _ will nev - er grow old.
3. *See Additional Lyrics*

Copyright © 1962 by Fort Knox Music Inc. and Trio Music Company
Copyright Renewed by Fort Knox Music Inc. and Arc Music Corporation (BMI)
International Copyright Secured   All Rights Reserved
Used by Permission

Additional Lyrics

3. Love you, baby, with all my might.
   Love like mine is outta sight.
   I'll lie for you if you want me to.
   I really don't believe that your love is true.

I'm Your Hoochie Coochie Man

Written by Willie Dixon

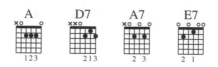

Strum Pattern: 9
Pick Pattern: 9

Verse
Moderately

1. The gyp-sy wom-an told my moth-er be-fore I was born,
2., 3. *See Additional Lyrics*

"You got a boy child com-in', goin' be a son of a gun." _

Gon-na make pret-ty wom-en _ jump and shout, _ then the world gon-na know

Chorus

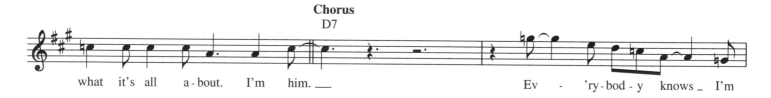

what it's all a-bout. I'm him. _ Ev-'ry-bod-y knows _ I'm

him. I'm the Hooch — ie Cooch-ie Man, _

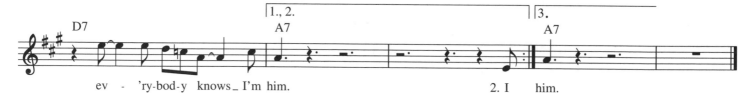

ev-'ry-bod-y knows _ I'm him. 2. I him.

Additional Lyrics

2. I got a black cat bone,
   I got a mojo too,
   I got the Johnny conkeroo,
   I'm gonna mess with you.
   I'm gonna make you girls
   Lead me by the hand,
   Then the world's gonna know,
   I'm that Hoochie Coochie Man.

3. On the seventh hour,
   On the seventh day,
   On the seventh month,
   The seventh doctor said:
   "He was born for good luck,"
   And that, you'll see,
   I got seven hundred dollars,
   Don't you mess with me.

© 1957 (Renewed 1985), 1964 HOOCHIE COOCHIE MUSIC (BMI)/Administered by BUG MUSIC
All Rights Reserved   Used by Permission

If You Love Me Like You Say

Words and Music by Little Johnny Taylor

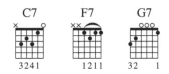

Strum Pattern: 6
Pick Pattern: 4

Additional Lyrics

2. Said you'd never run around.
   Said you'd never stay out late.
   Said you'd never run around.
   Said you'd never stay out late.
   Let me tell you pretty baby,
   I've got to set you straight.

Copyright © 1998 Cireco Music
International Copyright Secured   All Rights Reserved

It Hurts Me Too

Words and Music by Mel London

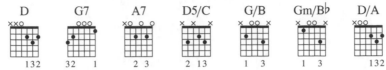

Strum Pattern: 1, 3
Pick Pattern: 1, 4

Copyright © 1957 (Renewed) by Conrad Music, a division of Arc Music Corp. (BMI) and Lonmel Publishing (BMI)
International Copyright Secured   All Rights Reserved
Used by Permission

It Serves Me Right to Suffer

Words and Music by John Lee Hooker

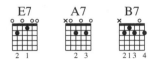

Strum Pattern: 1, 3
Pick Pattern: 1, 3

Verse
Slow Blues

1., 4. It serves me right to suf-fer, _   it serves me right   to be a - lone. ____
2., 3. *See Additional Lyrics*

It   serves me right   to suf-fer,   it serves me right   to be a - lone. _

Be - cause my mind, I'm still   liv - ing, the   days _ done passed and   gone. _

D.C. and Fade

Additional Lyrics

2. Every time I see a woman,
   And, folks, she makes me think of mine.
   Every time I see a woman,
   And, folks, she makes me think of mine.
   And that's why, that's why
   Folks, I just can't keep from crying.

3. My doctor put me on
   Milk, cream and alcohol.
   My doctor put me on, put me on,
   Milk, cream and alcohol.
   He said, "Johnny, your nerves are so bad,
   So bad, Johnny, until you just can't
   Sleep at night." (Oh yes, oh yes.)

Copyright © 1964 (Renewed) by Conrad Music, a division of Arc Music Corp. (BMI)
International Copyright Secured   All Rights Reserved
Used by Permission

Jailhouse Blues

Words and Music by Bessie Smith and Clarence Williams

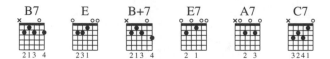

Strum Pattern: 1
Pick Pattern: 2

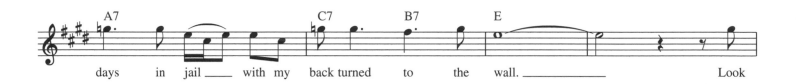

1. Thir-ty days in jail with my back turned to the wall, thir-ty
4. *See Additional Lyrics*

days in jail with my back turned to the wall. Look

here, mis-ter jail keep-er, put an-oth-er gal in my stall. 2. I don't

Verse

mind bein' in jail but I got-ta stay there so long, I don't
5. *See Additional Lyrics*

mind bein' in jail but I got-ta stay there so long. Ev - 'ry

friend I had, done shook hands and gone. 3. Bet - ter

© 1923 (Renewed) FRANK MUSIC CORP.
All Rights Reserved

Verse

stop your man from tick-ling me un-der my chin, _____ bet - ter

6. See Additional Lyrics

stop your man ___ from tick-ling me un-der my chin. _____ If he

keeps on ___ tick - ling I'm ___ goin' to lick him on ___ in. _____ Good _

Outro

morn - ing, blues, _ blues, how do you do? _____ Good

morn - ing, blues, _____ blues, how do you do? _____ I

just came _ here to have a few _ words _ with _ you. _____ ___

Additional Lyrics

4. When the blues first got on me,
   They poured like a shower of rain.
   When the blues first got on me,
   They poured like a shower of rain.
   And I cried all night,
   Honey, ain't that a shame.

5. I ain't gonna cry,
   I ain't gonna grieve or moan.
   I ain't gonna cry,
   I ain't gonna grieve or moan,
   I'm gonna take my friend's man,
   The one who's living next door.

6. Goin' up to the country,
   And I can't take you.
   Goin' up to the country,
   And I can't take you.
   Nothin' in the country,
   That a monkey man can do.

Key to the Highway

Words and Music by Big Bill Broonzy and Chas. Segar

Strum Pattern: 8
Pick Pattern: 8

Copyright © 1941, 1944 SONGS OF UNIVERSAL, INC.
Copyright Renewed
All Rights Reserved   Used by Permission

Kidney Stew Blues

Words and Music by Leona Blackman and Eddie Vinson

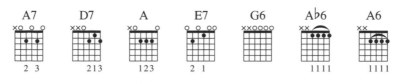

Strum Pattern: 1
Pick Pattern: 2, 5

Intro
Moderately

To Coda

Verse

1. Cra - zy 'bout you ba - by, but I just ain't got the price.
2., 3. *See additional lyrics*

Cra - zy 'bout you ba - by, but I just ain't got the price.

You're a high class ma - ma, so I guess it ain't no dice.

1., 2. | 3.

D.C. al Coda · Coda

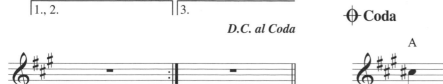

Additional Lyrics

2. Goin' back home, and get my old gal Sue.
   Goin' back home, and get my old gal Sue.
   She ain't the caviar kind,
   Just plain old kidney stew.

3. Old kidney stew, old kidney stew is fine.
   Old kidney stew, old kidney stew is fine.
   You can save your money,
   And keep your peace of mind.

© 1947 (Renewed) CHERIO CORP.
All Rights Reserved

Killing Floor

Words and Music by Chester Burnett

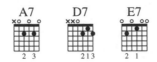

Strum Pattern: 1
Pick Pattern: 2

Verse

Fast Rock

I should-'ve quit you
Instrumental
long __ time a - go. __

I should-'ve quit you, ba - by, long __ time a - go. __ *Spoken: Yes, I*

should - 've, but you got me mess-in' a-round with you. Ba - by, you got me

cry - in' __ on the kill - ing floor. __ If I'd have fol-lowed you

my first night, __ if I'd have fol-lowed, pret - ty ba - by,

Copyright © 1965, 1970 (Renewed) by Arc Music Corporation (BMI)
International Copyright Secured   All Rights Reserved
Used by Permission

my first night, _____ I would-'ve been gone

since my sec - ond turn. *Spoken: Yeah.* Lord

Outro

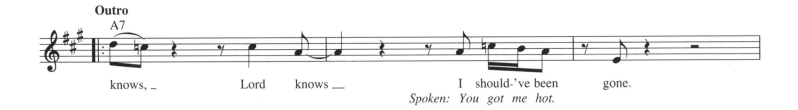
knows, _ Lord knows _ I should-'ve been gone.
Spoken: You got me hot.

Lord knows, _____ I should-'ve been gone.
You got me hot. *Ooh.* *You got me on you, babe. Ooh*

She got me mess - in' a - round with you, ba - by, you got me

cry - in' ___ on the kill - ing floor. _ *Spoken: Uh!* *That's all.*

Little Red Rooster

Written by Willie Dixon

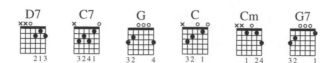

Strum Pattern: 2
Pick Pattern: 3

Intro
Slowly

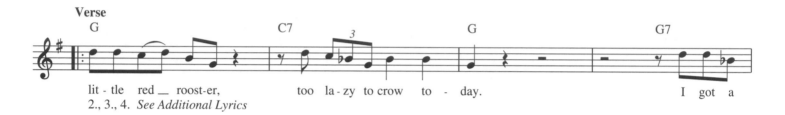

1. I got a

Verse

lit - tle red __ roost-er,   too la - zy to crow to - day.   I got a
2., 3., 4. *See Additional Lyrics*

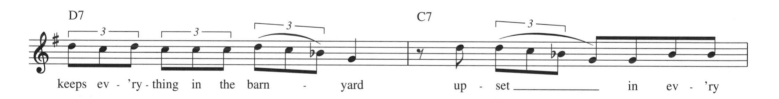

lit - tle red __ roost-er,   too la - zy to crow to - day.   He

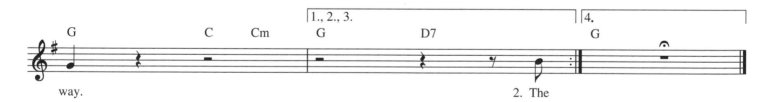

keeps ev - 'ry - thing in the barn - yard   up - set _____ in ev - 'ry

way.   2. The

Additional Lyrics

2. The dogs begin to bark, the hounds begin to howl.
   The dogs begin to bark, the hounds begin to howl.
   Watch out all you kinfolk, my little red rooster's on the prowl.

3. He keeps all the hens fighting among themselves.
   Tell you that he keeps all the hens fighting among themselves.
   He don't want no hens in the barnyard laying eggs for nobody else.

4. Now, if you see my red rooster, please send him home.
   Said if you see my red rooster, please send him home.
   I had no peace in the barnyard since the rooster's been gone.

© 1961 (Renewed 1989) HOOCHIE COOCHIE MUSIC (BMI) /Administered by BUG MUSIC
All Rights Reserved   Used by Permission

Love in Vain Blues

Words and Music by Robert Johnson

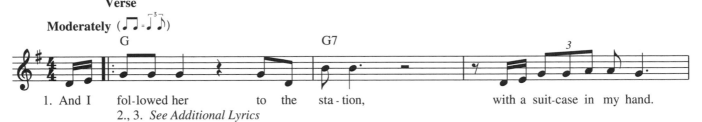

Strum Pattern: 1
Pick Pattern: 3

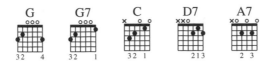

1. And I fol-lowed her to the sta-tion, with a suit-case in my hand.
2., 3. *See Additional Lyrics*

And I fol-lowed her to the sta-tion, with a suit-case in my hand.

Well, it's hard to tell, it's hard to tell, when all your love's in vain.

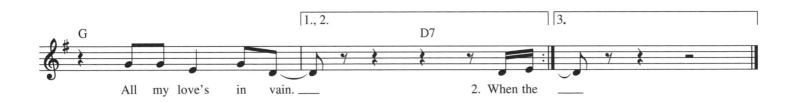

All my love's in vain. 2. When the

Additional Lyrics

2. When the train rolled up to the station, I looked her in the eye.
   When the train rolled up to the station, I looked her in the eye.
   Well, I was lonesome, I felt so lonesome, and I could not help but cry.
   All my love's in vain.

3. When the train, it left the station, with two lights on behind,
   When the train, it left the station, with two lights on behind,
   Well, the blue light was my blues, and the red light was my mind.
   All my love's in vain.

Copyright © (1978), 1990, 1991 MPCA King Of Spades (SESAC) and Claud L. Johnson
Administered by Music & Media International, Inc.
International Copyright Secured   All Rights Reserved

Love Struck Baby

Written by Stevie Ray Vaughan

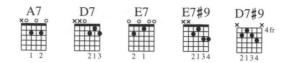

Strum Pattern: 1, 3
Pick Pattern: 2, 3
Verse
Moderately Fast

1. Well, I'm a love struck mm - ba - by. I must con - fess. ___ Life ___

___ with - out you darl - in', it's a sor - ry mess. _ Think - in' 'bout you ba - by, give me

such a thrill. _ I got - ta have you ___ ba - by, can't ___ get my fill. ___ I ___

___ love ya ba - by, and I know just what's to do. ___ I ___

Bridge

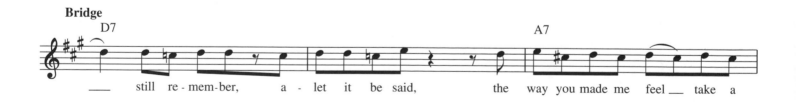

___ still re - mem - ber, a - let it be said, the way you made me feel ___ take a

fool to for - get. ___ I saw a ton o' bricks that hit me in the head ___ 'n' what ya

© 1983 STEVIE RAY SONGS (ASCAP)/Administered by BUG MUSIC
All Rights Reserved   Used by Permission

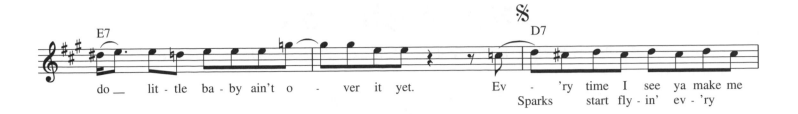

do __ lit-tle ba-by ain't o - ver it yet. Ev - 'ry time I see ya make me / Sparks start fly-in' ev - 'ry

feel so fine, __ my heart's beat-in' cra-zy my blood's __ run-nin' wild. Your / time we meet. __ Let me tell you ba-by, you knock me off my feet. Your

lov-in' make me feel __ like a might-y, might-y fine. Love __ me mm ba-by, I know __ / kiss-es, your lov - in', they're so God damn sweet. __ Don't-cha know mm ba-by, you can't __

Verse

__ you're mine. 2. I'm a / __ be beat. 3. Now I'm a } love struck ba-by. Yeah. I'm a love struck ba-by.

To Coda ⊕

You got me love struck mm ba-by, an' __ I know just what's to do. __

D.S. al Coda   ⊕ *Coda*

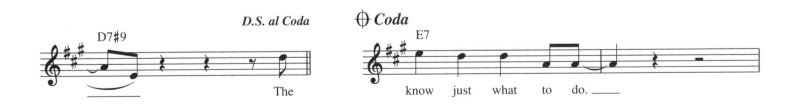

The / know just what to do. ____

Spoken: Ow!

Mannish Boy

Words and Music by McKinley Morganfield, Melvin London and Ellas McDaniel

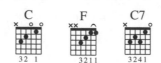

Strum Pattern: 9
Pick Pattern: 9

Intro
Moderate Blues

1. Now, when I was a young boy, at the age of five,
2., 3. *See Additional Lyrics*

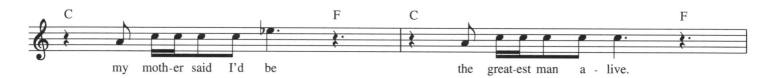

my moth-er said I'd be the great-est man a-live.

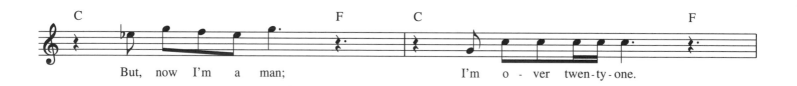

But, now I'm a man; I'm o-ver twen-ty-one.

You bet-ter be-lieve me, ba-by, I say we can have lots of fun.

Chorus

To Coda ⊕

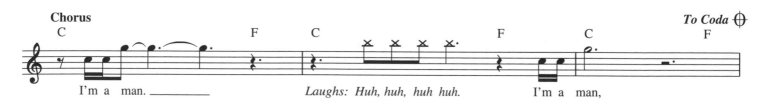

I'm a man. ___ *Laughs: Huh, huh, huh huh.* I'm a man,

oh yeah, oh yeah, ___ oh yeah, ___ oh yeah.

Copyright © 1955 (Renewed) by Arc Music Corporation (BMI), Lonmel Publishing (BMI) and Watertoons Music (BMI)/Administered by Bug Music
International Copyright Secured   All Rights Reserved
Used by Permission

Additional Lyrics

2. The night I shoot will never miss.
When I make love to you, baby,
You can't resist.
I'm a man; spelled M., A., (Child.)
N. No B., O., (Child.) Y.
That spells mannish boy.

3. All you pretty women,
Stand in line.
I'll make love to you, baby,
In an hour's time.
I'm a man, I'm a man,
Oh yeah, oh yeah,
Oh yeah, oh yeah.

Mary Had a Little Lamb

Written by Buddy Guy

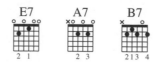

Strum Pattern: 1
Pick Pattern: 2

Verse
Moderately

1. Ma - ry had a lit - tle lamb, _ his fleece was white as snow, yeah.
2. *See Additional Lyrics*
3., 4., 5., 7. *Instrumental*

Ev - 'ry-where the child _ went, you know the lamb was sure ta go, yeah.

6. *Tis - ket,* tas - ket a green and yel - low bas - ket.

D.C. and Fade

Sent a let - ter to my ba - by, on my way I passed _ it.

Additional Lyrics

2. He followed her to school one day,
   And broke the teacher's rule.
   What a time did they have,
   That day at school.

© 1988 MIC-SHAU MUSIC (BMI) /Administered by BUG MUSIC
All Rights Reserved   Used by Permission

Mean Old World

Words and Music by Walter Jacobs

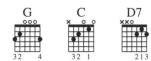

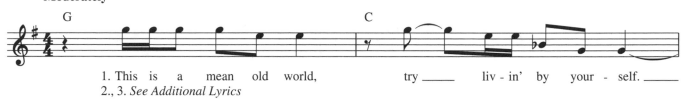

Strum Pattern: 1
Pick Pattern: 2

Verse
Moderately

1. This is a mean old world, try ___ liv-in' by your-self. ___
2., 3. *See Additional Lyrics*

___ This is a mean ___ old world,

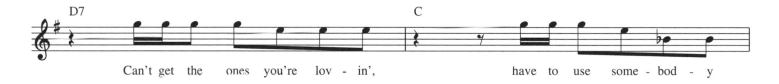

try ___ liv-in' by your-self. ___

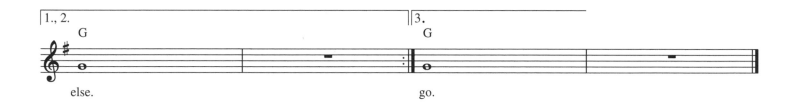

Can't get the ones you're lov-in', have to use some-bod-y

else.   go.

Additional Lyrics

2. I've got the blues, I'll pack my things and go.
   I've got the blues, I'll pack my things and go.
   I guess you don't love me, lucky Mister So and So.

3. Sometimes I wonder why can your love be so cold;
   Sometimes I wonder why can your love be so cold.
   Guess you don't love me, gonna pack my things and go.

Copyright © 1970 (Renewed) by Arc Music Corporation (BMI)
International Copyright Secured   All Rights Reserved
Used by Permission

Mean Mistreater

Words and Music by James Gordon

Strum Pattern: 1, 5
Pick Pattern: 1, 2

Chorus
Slow Blues

She's a mean mis-treat-er wom-an, she don't mean me ___ no ___ good. ___

She's ___ a mean mis-treat-in' wom-an, she don't mean me ___ no good. ___

Ring-in' door-bells on the av-e-nue ma-ma, ___

but I'd be the same way if I on-ly could. ___

Verse

1. You said ___ you were gon-na leave me, and you said you'd leave me soon. You
3. *See Additional Lyrics*

said you were gon-na leave me, ___ and ___ you were gon-na leave me soon. ___

But I had no i-de-a wom-an, that you meant to leave ___ at high noon. ___

Copyright © 1946 UNIVERSAL MUSIC CORP.
Copyright Renewed
All Rights Reserved Used by Permission

Chorus

You're a mean mis-treat-er, and you mis-treat-ed me all the time. _____ You're a

mean mis-treat - er, ___ 'cause you mis-treat-ed me all the _ time. _____ When I

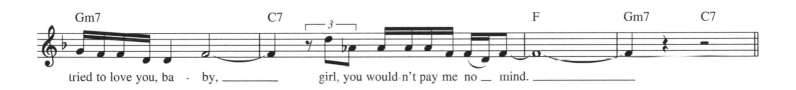

tried to love you, ba - by, _____ girl, you would-n't pay me no _ mind. _____

Verse

2., 4. Do you re-mem-ber the morn - in', ma - ma, ____ when I _ knocked on your door? _____

_____ Can't you re-mem - ber, ba - by, _ the morn-in' I knocked up-on your door? _____

You had the nerve_ to tell me, to tell me that you did-n't want me no more! _____

Additional Lyrics

3. Ain't it lost love livin' by yourself,
When the one that you're lovin',
Is lovin' someone else.
Ain't it lost love stayin' by yourself,
When there's one that you're lovin',
And she's lovin' someone else.

Mercury Blues

Written by K.C. Douglas and Robert Geddins

Strum Pattern: 1
Pick Pattern: 3

Additional Lyrics

2. Well, the girl I love,
   I stole her from an friend.
   He got lucky, stole her back again.
   She heard he had a Mercury,
   Lord, she's crazy 'bout a Mercury.
   I'm gonna buy me a Mercury
   And cruise it up and down the road.

3. Well, hey now mama,
   You look so fine
   Ridin' 'round in your Mercury '49.
   Crazy 'bout a Mercury,
   Lord, I'm crazy 'bout a Mercury.
   I'm gonna buy me a Mercury
   And cruise it up and down the road.

4. Well, my baby went out,
   She didn't stay long.
   Bought herself a Mercury, come a cruisin' home.
   She's crazy 'bout a Mercury,
   Yeah, she's crazy 'bout a Mercury.
   I'm gonna buy me a Mercury
   And cruise it up and down the road.

© 1970 (Renewed 1998) B-FLAT PUBLISHING and TRADITION MUSIC (BMI)/Administered by BUG MUSIC
All Rights Reserved   Used by Permission

My Babe

Written by Willie Dixon

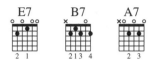

Strum Pattern: 3
Pick Pattern: 3

Verse
Moderate Blues

1. My ba - by don't stand no cheat - in', my babe.
2., 3., 4. *See Additional Lyrics*

My ba - by don't stand no cheat - in', my babe.

My ba - by don't stand no cheat-in', she don't stand none of that mid - night creep - in'.

My babe, true lit - tle ba - by, __ my babe.

Additional Lyrics

2. My babe, I know she love me, my babe.
   My babe, I know she love me, my babe.
   Oh yeah, I know she love me.
   She don't do nothing but kiss and hug me.
   My babe, true little baby, my babe.

3. My babe, she don't stand no cheatin', my babe.
   My babe, she don't stand no cheatin', my babe.
   Oh no, she don't stand no cheatin'.
   Ev'rything she do she do so pleasin'.
   My babe, true little baby, my babe.

4. My baby don't stand no fooling, my babe.
   My baby don't stand no fooling, my babe.
   My baby don't stand no foolin'.
   When she's hot there ain't no coolin'.
   My babe, true little baby, my babe.

© 1955 (Renewed 1983) HOOCHIE COOCHIE MUSIC (BMI) /Administered by BUG MUSIC
All Rights Reserved   Used by Permission

Milk Cow Blues

Words and Music by Kokomo Arnold

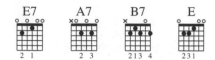

E7   A7   B7   E

Strum Pattern: 1
Pick Pattern: 6

Verse

Slow Blues Shuffle

1. Hol-ler-ing good morn-in'   I ___ said,   "Blues,_ how do you do?"

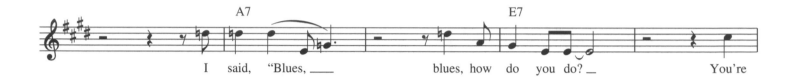

I said, "Blues, ___   blues, how do you do? _   You're

might-y ear-ly this morn - in', ___   and I can't get a - long ___ with you."   2. How

Verse

can I do right,_ ba - by,   when you won't do right your-self?   How can I

do right, ba - by,   when you won't do right your - self? ___   If

my good gal quits me, ___   Lord, I don't want no - bod - y else.   3. Well, I

Verse

woke up this morn-in',   looked out my door,   and I know my milk cow_   by the way she lows._ If you

Copyright © 1934 UNIVERSAL MUSIC CORP.
Copyright Renewed
All Rights Reserved   Used by Permission

see my milk cow, please drive her home. ___ I ain't

had no milk ___ and but - ter, ___ since that cow's ___ been gone. ___

Verse

4. My blues fell this morn - in', and my love ___ came fall - in' down. ___ Well,

my blues ___ fell this morn-in', and my love came fall - in' down. ___ I may

be a low-down _ dog, ma - ma, but _ please _ don't dog ___ me 'round. ___ 5. It ___ takes a

Verse

rock - in' chair to rock, a rub - ber ball to roll, takes a long tall sweet gal _ to ___

sat - is - fy my soul, Lord. I don't feel wel - come, no ___ place I go. ___

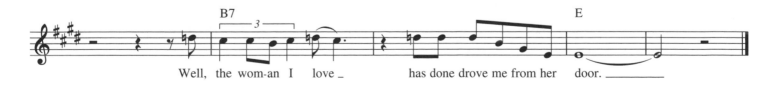

Well, the wom-an I love _ has done drove me from her door. ___

Nobody Knows You When You're Down and Out

Words and Music by Jimmie Cox

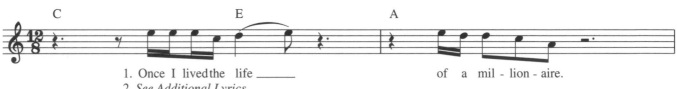

Strum Pattern: 8
Pick Pattern: 8

Verse
Slow Blues

1. Once I lived the life _____ of a mil - lion - aire.
2. *See Additional Lyrics*

Spent all my mon - ey; I just did not care.

Took all my friends ___ out ___ for a good time; ___

bought boot - leg whis - key, cham - pagne and wine. ___

Chorus

No, no, no - bod - y knows you

when you're down and out. ___ In your pock - et,

Copyright © 1923, 1929, 1950, 1959, 1963 JUNIVERSAL MUSIC CORP.
Copyright Renewed
All Rights Reserved   Used by Permisssion

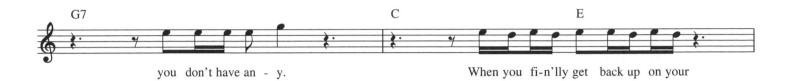

not one pen - ny.   And as for friends,

you don't have an - y.   When you fi-n'lly get back up on your

feet a - gain, ___   ev - 'ry-bod - y wants to be

your long lost friend.   Said, it's might - y strange, _

'out a doubt. ___   No - bod - y knows you,

no - bod - y knows, _   no - bod - y knows you

when you're down ___ and out.

Additional Lyrics

2. Then I began to fall so low.
   Lost all my good friends; I didn't have nowhere to go.
   I get my hands on a dollar again,
   I'm gonna hang on to it till the eagle grins, yeah.

One Bourbon, One Scotch, One Beer

Words and Music by John Lee Hooker

Strum Pattern: 3, 4
Pick Pattern: 1, 3

Copyright © 1967 (Renewed) by Conrad Music, a division of Arc Music Corporation (BMI)
International Copyright Secured   All Rights Reserved
Used by Permission

it was ten-thir-ty then.   I looked down at the bar

at the bar - ten-der.   Said...   He said, "What do ya want _ John-ny?"   One

Chorus

G7

bour-bon,   one scotch   and one   beer.

Additional Lyrics

3. Well my baby's been gone, she's been gone tonight
   I ain't seen my baby since night before last.
   I wanna get drunk, get her off a' my mind.

4. *Spoken:* And I sat there, gettin' high, stoned, knocked out,
   And by that time, I looked on the wall,
   At the old clock again, and by that time,
   It was quarter to two:
   Last call for alcohol.
   I said, "Hey Mr. Bartender!"
   "What do ya want?"

Pride and Joy

Written by Stevie Ray Vaughan

Strum Pattern: 3
Pick Pattern: 3

Verse
Moderate Blues Shuffle

E7

1. Well,   you've heard a - bout   love   giv-in' sight ___ to the   blind. _

My   ba-by's lov- in' 'cause the   sun   to   shine. _ She's my   sweet   lit-tle thing, _

© 1985 RAY VAUGHAN MUSIC (ASCAP)/Administered by BUG MUSIC
All Rights Reserved   Used by Permission

she's   my   pride   and   joy. ___   She's   my

sweet   lit - tle   ba - by,   I'm ___ her ___ lit - tle   lov - er   boy. ___

Verse

2. Yeah,   I   love   my   la - dy   to   be   long   and   lean, ___
3., 4. *See Additional Lyrics*

you   mess   with   her,   you'll   see   a   man   get - tin'   mean. ___   She's   my

sweet   lit - tle   thing, ___   she's   my   pride   and   joy. ___

She's   my   sweet   lit - tle   ba - by,   I'm ___ her ___ lit - tle   lov - er

boy. ___   3. Yeah,   I   4. Yeah,   I

Additional Lyrics

3. Yeah, I love my baby like the finest wine;
   Stick with her until the end of time.
   She's my sweet little thing,
   She's my pride and joy.
   She's my sweet little baby,
   I'm her little lover boy.

4. Yeah, I love my baby, my heart and soul;
   Love like ours won't never grow old.
   She's my sweet little thing,
   She's my pride and joy.
   She's my sweet little baby,
   I'm her little lover boy.

Ramblin' on My Mind

Words and Music by Robert Johnson

Strum Pattern: 1
Pick Pattern: 2

Additional Lyrics

2. I'm goin' down to the station, catch that old fast milk train, you'll see.
   I'm goin' down to the station, catch that old fast milk train, you'll see.
   I've got the blues 'bout Miss So and So, and the sun got the blues 'bout me.

3. I got mean things, I've got mean things all on my mind.
   Little girl, little girl, I've got mean things all on my mind.
   Is to leave my baby, 'cause she treat me so unkind.

Copyright © (1978), 1990, 1991 MPCA King Of Spades (SESAC) and Claud L. Johnson
Administered by Music & Media International, Inc.
International Copyright Secured   All Rights Reserved

Pinetop's Blues

Words and Music by Pinetop Smith

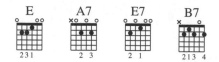

Strum Pattern: 1
Pick Pattern: 3

Verse
Moderate Blues Shuffle

1. Now my wom - an's got a heart like a rock ___ cast down in ___ the sea,

___ now my wom - an's got a heart like a rock ___ cast down in ___ the sea. _

___ She thinks she can love ev - 'ry - bod - y ___ and ___

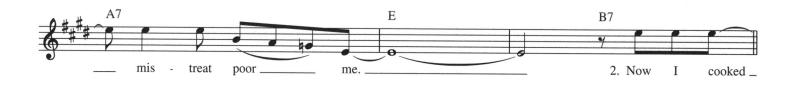

___ mis - treat poor ___ me. ___ 2. Now I cooked _

Verse

___ her break - fast, _ e - ven car - ried it to ___ her bed, ___ now I cooked _

___ her break - fast, _ e - ven car - ried it to ___ her bed. ___ Now she took _

Copyright © 1929, 1941 UNIVERSAL MUSIC CORP.
Copyright Renewed
All Rights Reserved   Used by Permission

_____ one bite _____ and threw the tea cup at poor Pine-top's head. _____ 3. I'm gon - na

Verse

buy my - self _____ a grave - yard of _____ my own. _____ I'm gon - na

buy my - self _____ a grave - yard of _____ my own. _____ I'm gon - na

bur - y that wom - an if she don't let me a - lone. _____ 4. I can't use _____

Verse

_____ no wom - an _____ if she can't help me lose _____ the blues. _____ I can't use _____

_____ no wom - an _____ if she can't help me lose _____ the blues. _____ Go - in' down _____

_____ on State Street _____ just to buy _____ me a gal - lon of booze. _____

Please Send Me Someone to Love

Words and Music by Percy Mayfield

Copyright © 1950, 1951 Sony/ATV Music Publishing LLC
Copyright Renewed
All Rights Administered by Sony/ATV Music Publishing LLC, 8 Music Square West, Nashville, TN 37203
International Copyright Secured   All Rights Reserved

Bridge

wake nights _ and pon - der _ world trou - bles. _ My an - swer _ is al - ways _ the

same. _____ That un - less men _ put an end _____ to all of this, _____

hate will put the world _____ in a flame, _____ what a shame. _____ 3. Just be -

Verse

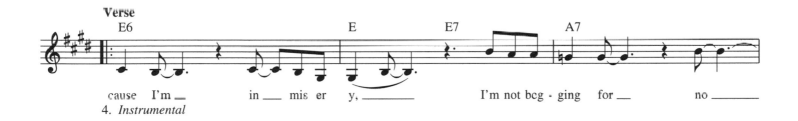

cause I'm _ in _ mis er y, _____ I'm not beg - ging for _ no _____
4. *Instrumental*

_ sym - pa - thy. But, if it's not _____ ask - ing too much, _ please send me some-one

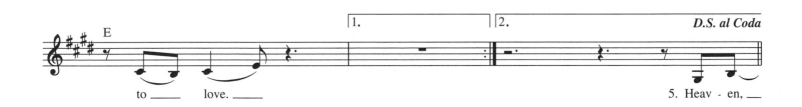

to _____ love. _____   5. Heav - en, _

⊕ Coda

not _ ask - ing too much, _ please _ send me some-one _ to love. Hmm. _____

Reconsider Baby

Words and Music by Lowell Fulson

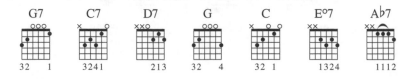

Additional Lyrics

3. You said you once had loved me, but now I guess you have changed your mind.
   You said you once had loved me, but now I guess you have changed your mind.
   Why don't you reconsider, baby, give yourself just a little more time.

Copyright © 1955, 1964 (Renewed) by Arc Music Corporation (BMI)
International Copyright Secured   All Rights Reserved
Used by Permission

Rock Me Baby

Words and Music by B.B. King and Joe Bihari

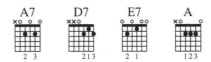

Strum Pattern: 1
Pick Pattern: 1

Chorus
Moderate Blues Shuffle

Rock me ba - by, rock me all night long. _____
See Additional Lyrics

Rock me ba - by, rock me _____ all _____ night long. _____

I want you to rock me ba - by, like my back ain't got no bone. _____

Verse

1., 2. Roll me ba - by, like you roll a wag - on wheel.

Roll me ba - by, like you roll a wag - on wheel. I want you to

roll me ba - by, _____ you don't know how it makes me feel.

Additional Lyrics

Chorus Rock me baby, honey rock me slow.
Rock me baby, honey rock me slow.
Rock me baby, till I want no more.

Copyright © 1964 by Universal Music - Careers
Copyright Renewed
International Copyright Secured All Rights Reserved

Rollin' Stone
(Catfish Blues)

Written by McKinley Morganfield (Muddy Waters)

E7

Strum Pattern: 1
Pick Pattern: 2

Verse
Moderate Blues

1. Well, I wished _ I was a cat - fish, swim-min' in the _
2., 3., 4. *See Additional Lyrics*

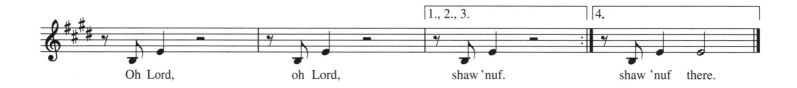

_____ deep blue sea. _____ I would have all ___ you good look-in' wom-en fish-in',

fish - in' af - ter me. Shaw 'nuf af-ter me, shaw 'nuf af - ter me.

Oh Lord, oh Lord, shaw 'nuf. shaw 'nuf there.

1., 2., 3.　　4.

Additional Lyrics

2. I went my baby's house, and I sit down on her sill.
   She said, "Come on in, Muddy, my mother's just not well."
   Shaw 'nuf, just not well, shaw 'nuf, just not well.
   Oh, Lord, oh, well.

3. Well, my mother told my father just before I was born,
   "I got a boy child comin', gonna be a rolling stone."
   Shaw 'nuf he's a rolling stone. Shaw 'nuf he's a rolling stone. Shaw 'nuf he's a rolling stone.
   Oh, well, he's a. Oh, well, he's a. Oh, well, he's a...

4. Well, I feel, yes, I feel, baby, like my lowdown time ain't long.
   I'm gonna cut the twist train, Spokane bound.
   Back down the road I'm goin', boy.
   Shaw 'nuf there. Shaw 'nuf there. Shaw 'nuf there.

© 1960 (Renewed 1988) WATERTOONS MUSIC (BMI) /Administered by BUG MUSIC
All Rights Reserved   Used by Permission

See See Rider

Words and Music by Ma Rainey

Strum Pattern: 1, 6
Pick Pattern: 1, 2

Intro
Moderate Blues

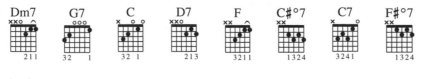

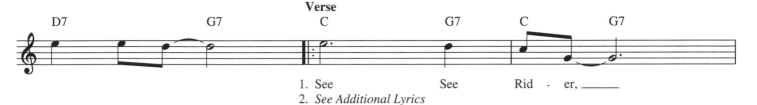

Verse

1. See   See   Rid - er, _____
2. *See Additional Lyrics*

see   what   you   have   done. ___ Law'd,   Law'd,   Law'd,   made   me   love   you,

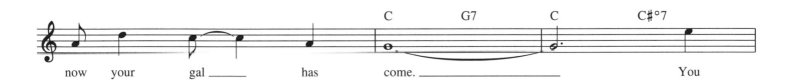

now   your   gal _____ has   come. _____ You

made   me   love ___ you,   now   your   gal   has   come. _____

___   I'm   goin' _____ a - way, ___ ba - by. ___

I   won't   be   back   'til   fall. _____ Law'd,   Law'd, ___ Law'd,

goin'   a - way,   ba - by,   won't   be   back   'til   fall. _____

Copyright © 1943, 1944 UNIVERSAL MUSIC CORP.
Copyrights Renewed
All Rights Reserved   Used by Permission

If I find me a good man, won't be back __ at

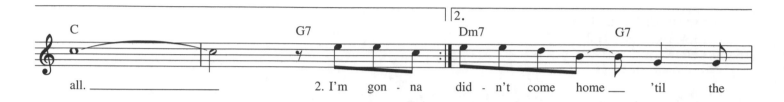

all. _____ 2. I'm gon - na did - n't come home __ 'til the

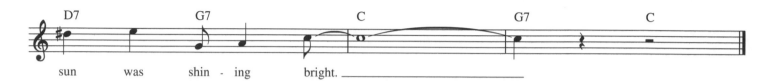

sun was shin - ing bright. _____

Additional Lyrics

2. I'm gonna buy me a pistol just as long as I am tall.
   Law'd, Law'd, Law'd, shoot my man and catch a Cannonball.
   If he won't have me, he won't have no gal at all.
   See See Rider, where did you stay last night?
   Law'd, Law'd, Law'd, your shoes ain't buttoned, your clothes don't fit you right.
   You didn't come home 'til the sun was shining bright.

The Seventh Son

Written by Willie Dixon

Strum Pattern: 3
Pick Pattern: 3

Intro
Moderately

Ev - 'ry - bod - y's talk - in' 'bout the sev - enth son. __ In the

Chorus

whole round world there is on - ly one. And I'm the one,

I'm the one, __ I'm the one, I'm the one, __ the

© 1955 (Renewed 1983) HOOCHIE COOCHIE MUSIC (BMI) /Administered by BUG MUSIC
All Rights Reserved   Used by Permission

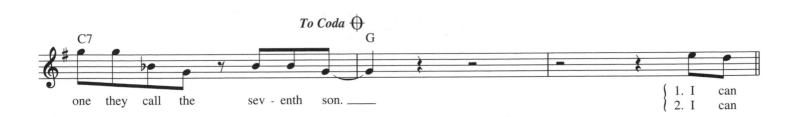

one they call the sev - enth son. _____

1. I can
2. I can

1. **Verse**

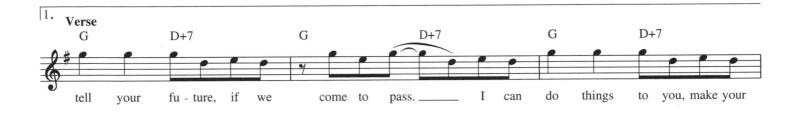

tell your fu - ture, if we come to pass. _____ I can do things to you, make your

heart feel glad; look in the sky, pre - dict the rain, _

2.
Verse

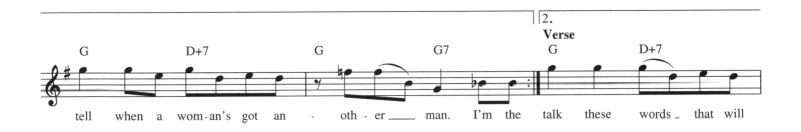

tell when a wom-an's got an - oth - er _____ man. I'm the talk these words _ that will

sound so sweet, _ they will e - ven make your lit - tle heart _ skip a beat;

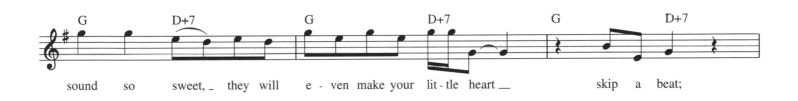

heal the sick, raise the dead, _ make the lit - tle girls _ talk

D.S. al Coda   ⊕ **Coda**

out of their heads. _ I'm the

_____

Route 66

By Bobby Troup

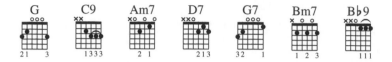

Strum Pattern: 3
Pick Pattern: 3

Moderately Bright

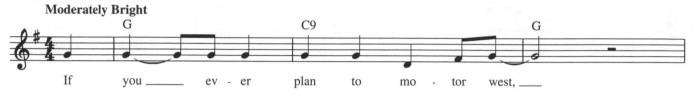

If you _____ ev - er plan to mo - tor west, _____

trav - el my way, take the high - way that's the best. _

_ Get your kicks on Route _ Six - ty - six! _

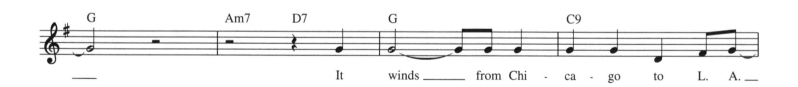

_ It winds _____ from Chi - ca - go to L. A. _

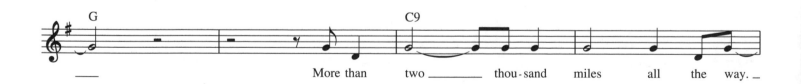

_ More than two _____ thou - sand miles all the way. _

_ Get your kicks on Route _ Six - ty - six! _

Copyright © 1946, Renewed 1973, Assigned 1974 to Londontown Music
All Rights outside the U.S.A. controlled by E.H. Morris & Company
International Copyright Secured   All Rights Reserved

Now you go thru Saint Loo - ey and

Jop - lin, Mis - sour - i and Ok - la - hom - a Cit - y is might - y pret - ty; you'll see

Am - ar - il - lo; Gal - up, New

Mex - i - co; Flag - staff, Ar - i - zon - a; don't for - get Wi - no - na,

King - man, Bar - stow, San - Ber - nar - din - o. Won't you get hip

to this time - ly tip: When you

make that Cal - i - for - nia trip get your

kicks on Route Six - ty - six!

Sitting on Top of the World

Words and Music by Chester Burnett

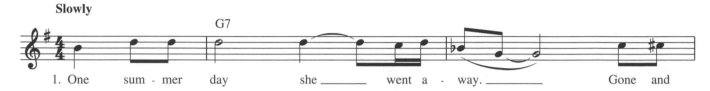

Strum Pattern: 3
Pick Pattern: 3

1. One sum - mer day she _____ went a - way. _____ Gone and

left me, gone to stay. She's gone but I don't

wor - ry _____ 'cause I'm sit - tin' on top _____ of the world. _____

2. All the sum - mer, _____ worked on this farm. _____ Had to take

Christ - mas _____ in my o - ver - all. _____ She's gone, but I

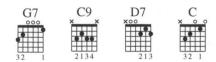

don't _ wor - ry, 'cause I'm sit - tin', sit - tin' on top of the world. _____

Copyright © 1958 (Renewed) by Arc Music Corporation (BMI)
International Copyright Secured   All Rights Reserved
Used by Permission

Spoonful

Written by Willie Dixon

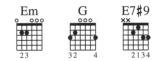

Strum Pattern: 1
Pick Pattern: 2

Verse
Moderate Shuffle

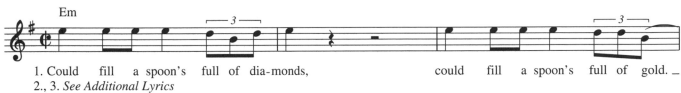

1. Could fill a spoon's full of dia-monds, could fill a spoon's full of gold. _
2., 3. *See Additional Lyrics*

_ Just a _ lit-tle spoon of your _ pre-cious love _

sat - is - fy _ my soul. _ Men _ lies _ a - bout it;

some of them cries _ a - bout it. Some of them

dies _ a - bout it. Ev - 'ry-thing's a - fight-in' a - bout the

spoon - ful. _ That spoon, that spoon, that spoon - ful. _ That spoon, that spoon, that

spoon - ful. _ That spoon, that spoon, that spoon - ful. _ That spoon, that spoon, that

© 1960 (Renewed 1988) HOOCHIE COOCHIE MUSIC (BMI) /Administered by BUG MUSIC
All Rights Reserved   Used by Permission

Interlude

spoon.

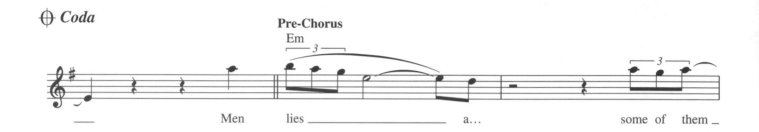

Coda

Pre-Chorus

Men   lies _____ a…   some of them _

_ cries _____ a - bout _ it. _   Some of them   dies. _____

Ev - 'ry-thing's a - fight-in' a - bout it, uh. _   Ev - 'ry-thing's a -

cry - in' a - bout it, _____ uh.   Ev - 'ry - thing's a,   ev - 'ry-thing's a -

die - in' a - bout it.   Ev - 'ry-thing's a - cry - in' a - bout it.   Ev - 'ry-thing's a -

ly - in' a - bout it. _____   Li'l' old, _____ li'l' old,

spoon - ful, __ spoon - ful. ____

Hey! ____ Ev - 'ry - thing's _ die-in' a-bout it, uh.

Chorus

Em

All right, just cry-in' a-bout it. ____ That spoon, that spoon, that

lit - tle old spoon, __ lit - tle old spoon, __ lit - tle old

lit - tle old spoon, __ lit - tle old spoon, __ lit - tle old

spoon - ful. __ That spoon, that spoon, that spoon - ful. __ Spoon, that spoon, that

spoon - ful. __ Yeah. ____

Freely

N.C. G E7#9

Ev - 'ry-thing's a - die-in' a-bout it. ____ Hey! ____

Additional Lyrics

2. Could fill a spoon's full of coffee;
   Could fill a spoon's full of tea.
   Just a little spoon of your precious love,
   Is that enough for me?

3. Could fill a spoon's full of water,
   Saved them from the desert sands.
   Was a little spoon of your love, baby,
   Saved you from another man.

Statesboro Blues

Words and Music by Willy McTell

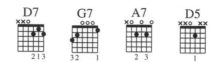

Strum Pattern: 1, 6
Pick Pattern: 2, 6

1. Wake up, ma-ma, turn your lamp down low. ___

Wake up, ma-ma, ___ turn your lamp down low. Ya

got no nerve ___ ba-by, ya turn Un-cle John from your ___ door.

2. I woke up this morn-in' an' I had them States-bo-ro blues. ___

I woke up this morn-in' an' I had them States-bo-ro blues. ___ Well, I looked

o-ver in the cor-ner, ba-by, your grand-pa ___ seem to have them, too. Oh!

Copyright © 1929 by Peer International Corporation
Copyright Renewed
International Copyright Secured   All Rights Reserved

Interlude

D7 G7 D7 G7 D7 A7

3. Well, my

Verse

D7

ma-ma died and left me, my pa-pa died and left me. I ain't good look-in', ba-by, want

G7

some-one sweet and __ kind. ____ I'm go-in' to the coun-try, ba-by, do you wan-na go? __

D7 A7

____ If you can't make it, ba-by,

G7 D7

your sis-ter Lu-cille said she wan-na go. *Spoken: Well, I sho' nuff tell ya...*

Interlude

D7 G7 D7 G7 D7 A7

Verse

D7 G7 D7

4. I love that wom - an bet-ter 'n an - y wom-an I've ev-er seen. ____

G7

Well, I ____ love that wom - an, bet-ter 'n an - y wom-an I've ev-er

D7 A7

seen. Well, she treat me like a king, ____ yeah, yeah,

95

Texas Flood

Words and Music by Larry Davis and Joseph W. Scott

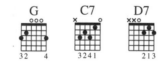

Strum Pattern: 7
Pick Pattern: 7

Verse
Slow Blues

Copyright © 1958 SONGS OF UNIVERSAL, INC. and FLOREE MUSIC COMPANY
Copyright Renewed
All Rights Reserved   Used by Permission

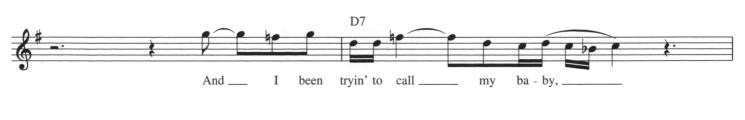

And __ I been tryin' to call _____ my ba - by, _____

Lord, _ now I can't get a sin - gle sound.   2. Well, _ dark

Verse

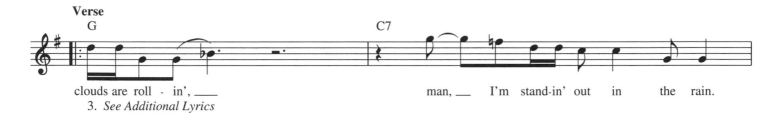

clouds are roll - in', ____   man, __ I'm stand-in' out in the rain.
3. *See Additional Lyrics*

Well, __ dark   clouds are roll - in', ____

man, ____ I'm stand - in' out in the rain.

Yeah,   flood - wa - ter keep roll   -   in',

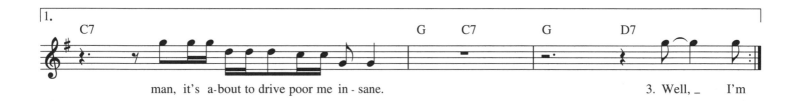

man, it's a-bout to drive poor me in - sane.   3. Well, _ I'm

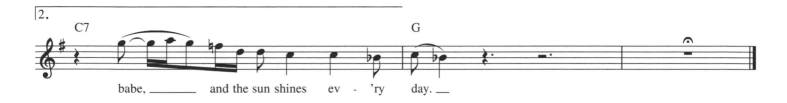

babe, _____ and the sun shines ev - 'ry day. __

Additional Lyrics

3. Well, I'm leavin' you baby,
   Lord, now I'm goin' back home to stay.
   Well, back home there's no floods, or tornadoes, babe,
   And the sun shines ev'ry day.

Stella Mae

Words and Music by John Lee Hooker

Strum Pattern: 1, 3
Pick Pattern: 2, 3

Verse
Moderate Shuffle

1. Stel-la Mae,   I love you, ba-by.   Stel-la
2.-5. *See Additional Lyrics*

Mae,   I love you,_ ba - by.   I'd do an - y-thing   you asked me

to, 'cause I love _____ you.   2. Stel - la

Ba - by!   Oo, _____

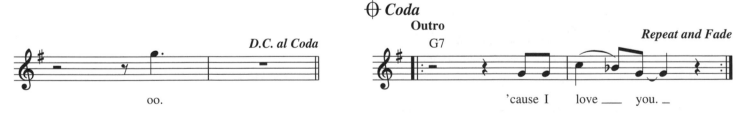

oo.   'cause I love ___ you. _

Additional Lyrics

2. Stella Mae, you changed my drink, to milk and creme.
I did it, I did it, just for you,
'Cause I love you. I love you Stella Mae.
I'd do anything for you, 'cause I love you.

3. Now, Stella Mae, if you told me to jump in the ocean,
I know I can't swim, but I'd try to do it just for you.
Because I love you, I love you, Stella Mae.

4. Now, baby, you made me stop gambling;
You made me stop staying up all night long.
Now, Stella Mae, I did all these things, I did them just for you.
'Cause I love you, I love you, oh yeah.

5. Now Stella Mae, if I had my choice for the whole round world,
I, I, baby, I'd tell you to be my choice
'Cause I love you, 'cause I love you, 'cause I love you.

Copyright © 1967 (Renewed) by Arc Music Corporation (BMI)
International Copyright Secured   All Rights Reserved
Used by Permission

Stormy Weather
(Keeps Rainin' All the Time)

from COTTON CLUB PARADE OF 1933

Lyric by Ted Koehler
Music by Harold Arlen

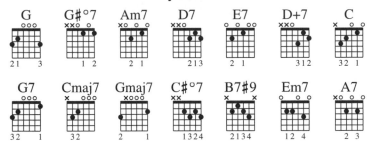

Strum Pattern: 4
Pick Pattern: 4

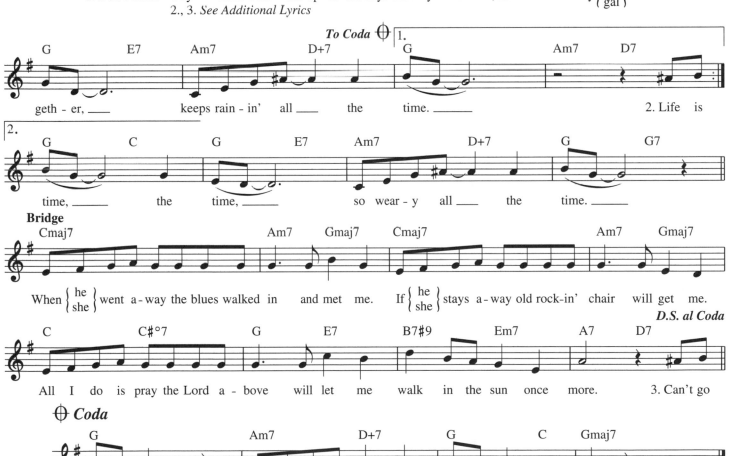

Additional Lyrics

2. Life is bare, gloom and mis'ry ev'rywhere.
   Stormy weather, just can't get my poor self together.
   I'm weary all the time, the time,
   So weary all the time.

3. Can't go on, ev'rything I had is gone.
   Stormy weather, since my { man / gal } and I ain't together,
   Keeps rainin' all the time,
   Keeps rainin' all the time.

© 1933 (Renewed 1961) FRED AHLERT MUSIC GROUP (ASCAP),
TED KOEHLER MUSIC CO. (ASCAP)/Administered by BUG MUSIC and S.A. MUSIC CO.
All Rights Reserved   Used by Permission

Sweet Home Chicago

Words and Music by Robert Johnson

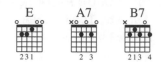

Strum Pattern: 3, 4
Pick Pattern: 3, 4

Intro

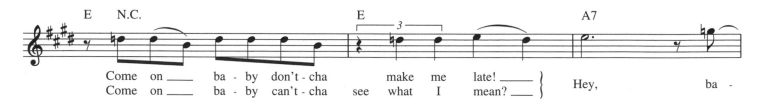

Copyright © (1978), 1990, 1991 MPCA King Of Spades Music (SESAC) and Claud L. Johnson
Administered by Music & Media International, Inc.
International Copyright Secured   All Rights Reserved

Sweet Sixteen

Words and Music by B.B. King and Joe Bihari

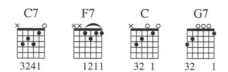

Strum Pattern: 1
Pick Pattern: 3

Verse
Moderate Blues shuffle

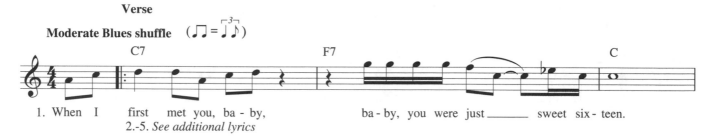

1. When I first met you, ba - by, ba - by, you were just _____ sweet six - teen.
2.-5. *See additional lyrics*

When I first met you, ba - by, ba - by, you were just _____ sweet six -

teen. _____ You just left your home then, wom - an,

oh, _____ the sweet - est thing I'd ev - er seen. _____ 2. But you _____

Additional Lyrics

2. But you wouldn't do nothing, babe, you wouldn't do anything I ask you to.
   You wouldn't do nothing for me, baby, you wouldn't do anything I asked you to.
   You know you ran away from your home, baby, you want to run away from me.

3. You know I love you, baby, and I'll do anything you tell me to.
   You know I love you, baby, and I'll do anything you tell me to.
   There ain't nothing in the world, woman, that I wouldn't do for you.

4. I just got back from Vietnam, and I'm a long way from New Orleans.
   I just got back from Vietnam, and I'm a long way from New Orleans.
   I'm having so much trouble, baby, I wonder what in the world is gonna happen to me.

5. Treat me mean, baby, but I'll keep on loving you.
   You can treat me mean, baby, but I'll keep loving you just the same.
   But one of these days, baby, you're gonna give a lot of money to hear someone call my name.

Copyright © 1967 by Universal Music - Careers
Copyright Renewed
International Copyright Secured All Rights Reserved

The Things That I Used to Do

Words and Music by Eddie "Guitar Slim" Jones

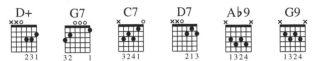

Strum Pattern: 7
Pick Pattern: 7

Intro
Moderately Slow

1. The things that I used to do, _____

Verse

Lord, _ I won't do no more. _____

3. *Instrumental*

The things that I used to do, _____ Lord, I won't do no

more. _____ I used to sit a-round do-in' noth-in', ah,

cry _____ ba-by, do not go. _____
2. I used to
4. *See Additional Lyrics*

Verse

search all _ night for ya, darl-in', Lord, an' my search would al-ways end in vain. _

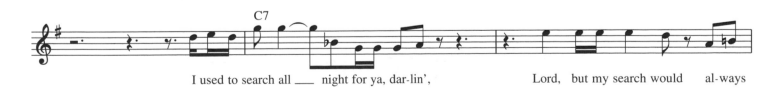

I used to search all _ night for ya, dar-lin', Lord, but my search would al-ways

Copyright © 1953 Sony/ATV Music Publishing LLC
Copyright Renewed
All Rights Administered by Sony/ATV Music Publishing LLC, 8 Music Square West, Nashville, TN 37203
International Copyright Secured   All Rights Reserved

To Coda ⊕

G7 ... D7

end in vain. ____ But I knew all the time dar-lin' _ ah,

D.S. al Coda

C7 ... G7 ... D7

that you was hid out with your oth-er man. ____

⊕ *Coda*

C7 N.C. ... G7 ... C7 ... G7 A♭9 G9

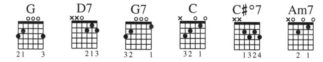

oh, _____ I just _ can't get a-long with you. ____

Additional Lyrics

4. I'm gon' send you back to yo' mama, darlin',
   Lord, 'n' I'm goin' back to my fam'ly, too.
   I'm gon' send you back to yo' mama, darlin,'
   Lord, 'n' I'm goin' back to my fam'ly, too.
   There's nothin' I can do to please ya, darlin', ah,
   Oh, I just can't get along with you.

Trouble in Mind

Words and Music by Richard M. Jones

G D7 G7 C C#°7 Am7

Strum Pattern: 4
Pick Pattern: 3
Verse
Slow Blues

G ... D7 ... G7

1. Trou-ble in mind, I'm blue. but I won't be blue al-

C C#°7 ... G ... Am7 ... D7

ways. For the sun will shine ___ in my back door some-day. _

G G7 Am7 D7 ... G ... D7

____ Trou-ble in mind, that's true, I have

Copyright © 1926, 1937 UNIVERSAL MUSIC CORP.
Copyright Renewed
All Rights Reserved   Used by Permission

al - most lost my mind. Life ain't worth liv - in, _____

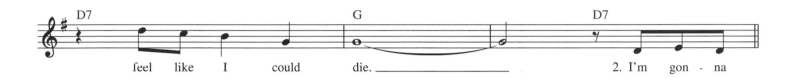

feel like I could die. _____ 2. I'm gon - na

Verse

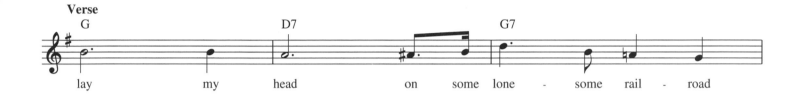

lay my head on some lone - some rail - road

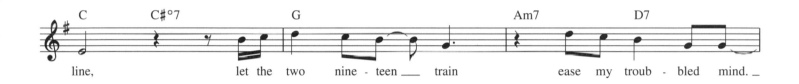

line, let the two nine - teen ___ train ease my troub - bled mind. _

_____ Trou - ble in mind, ___ I am

blue. My poor heart is beat - in' ___ slow. _____

Nev-er had no trou - ble in my life ___ be - fore. _____

Three O'Clock Blues

Words and Music by B.B. King and Jules Bihari

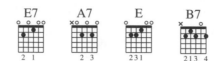

Strum Pattern: 8
Pick Pattern: 8

Moderately

Verse

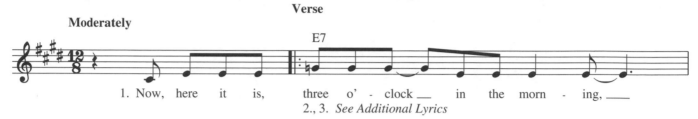

1. Now, here it is, three o'-clock in the morn - ing,
2., 3. *See Additional Lyrics*

and I can't e - ven close my eyes.

Oh yes, it's three o'-clock in the morn - ing ba - by,

I can't e - ven close my eyes. Well, I

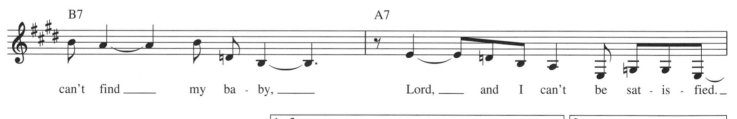

can't find my ba - by, Lord, and I can't be sat - is - fied.

1., 2. **3.**

2. I've looked a - round

Additional Lyrics

2. I've looked around me, people, and my baby knows she can't be found.
   I've looked around me, people, and my baby knows she can't be found.
   Well, you know if I don't find my baby, I'm going down to the Golden Ground.

3. Goodbye ev'rybody, I believe this is the end.
   Goodbye ev'rybody, I believe this is the end.
   I want you to tell my baby to forgive me for my sins.

Copyright © 1952 Universal Music - Careers
Copyright Renewed
International Copyright Secured   All Rights Reserved

The Thrill Is Gone

Words and Music by Roy Hawkins and Rick Darnell

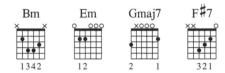

Strum Pattern: 1, 3
Pick Pattern: 2, 5

Verse
Moderately slow

1. The thrill is gone, the thrill is gone a-way.
2., 3., 4. *See additional lyrics*

The thrill is gone, ba-by, the thrill is gone

a - way. You know you done me wrong, ba-

- by, and you'll be sor - ry some-day.

Additional Lyrics

2. The thrill is gone, it's gone away from me.
The thrill is gone, it's gone away from me.
Although I still live on,
But so lonely I'll be.

3. The thrill is gone, it's gone away for good.
The thrill is gone, it's gone away for good.
Someday I know I'll be over it all, baby,
Just like I know a good man should.

3. You know I'm free, free now, baby, I'm free from your spell.
I'm free, free, free now, I'm free from your spell.
And now that it's all over,
All I can do is wish you well.

Copyright © 1951 by Universal Music - Careers
Copyright Renewed
International Copyright Secured All Rights Reserved

Walkin' Blues

Words and Music by Robert Johnson

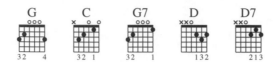

Strum Pattern: 1
Pick Pattern: 2

Verse
Moderate Slow Blues

1. Woke up this morn - in', feel 'round for my shoes. You know a-bout that, babe,
2., 3. *See Additional Lyrics*

I have that old walk-in' blues. Woke up this morn - in', I feel 'round for my

shoes. You know 'bout that ba - by, whoa,

Lord, I had them old walk - in' blues.

Additional Lyrics

2. I'm leavin' this mornin' I have to go ride the blinds.
I been mistreated. I don't mind dyin'
This a-mornin', if I have to go rob ya blind.
I been mistreated, whoa, Lord, I don't mind dyin'.

3. People tell me the walkin' blues ain't bad,
The worse old feelin' I most ever had.
People tell me the old walkin' blues ain't bad.
Well, it's the worse old feelin', whoa, Lord, the most I ever had.

Copyright © (1978), 1990, 1991 Lehsem II, LLC and Claud L. Johnson
Administered by Music & Media International, Inc.
International Copyright Secured   All Rights Reserved

Woke Up This Morning

Words and Music by Riley B. King and Jules Bihari

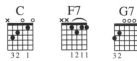

Strum Pattern: 3, 6
Pick Pattern: 3, 5

Additional Lyrics

2. I ain't got nobody to stay home with me.
   I ain't got nobody stayin' home with me.
   My baby, she's gone. I'm in misery.

4. Oo, I'm all alone.
   Oh, babe, I'm all alone.
   I ain't had no loving since my baby's been gone.

5. Whoa, baby, come on, stay with me.
   Oh, baby, come on, stay with me.
   My baby, she's gone. I'm in misery.

6. Whoa baby, take a swing with me.
   Whoa baby, take a swing with me.
   My baby, she's gone. My baby, she's gone.

Copyright © 1951 by Universal Music - Careers
Copyright Renewed
International Copyright Secured   All Rights Reserved

Who Do You Love

Words and Music by Ellas McDaniel

Strum Pattern: 3, 6
Pick Pattern: 3, 5

co - bra snake for a neck - tie. Got a brand new house on the road - side ___

made from rat - tle-snake hide. I got a brand new chim - ney made on top,

made from a hu - man skull. Now come on, ba - by, let's

take a lit - tle walk and tell me who do you love? ___

Copyright © 1956 (Renewed) by Arc Music Corporation (BMI)
International Copyright Secured   All Rights Reserved
Used by Permission

Ar - lene took me by the hand, _ she said, "Oo - ee, dad - dy, I un - der - stand."

play 3 times

Who do you love? ___ Who do you love? ___ 2. The

Verse
G5

night was black and the night was blue _ and a - round the cor - ner an ice wag - on flew. A

bump was hit and some - bod - y screamed. You should have heard just what I seen. Now

Outro-Chorus
G5

play 3 times

who do you love? ___ Who do you love? ___ I got a

G5

tomb - stone hand, a grave - yard mine. I lived long e - nough and I ain't scared o' dy - in'.

play 3 times

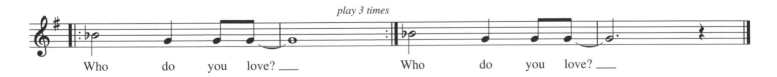

Who do you love? ___ Who do you love? ___

Worried Life Blues

Words and Music By Maceo Merriweather

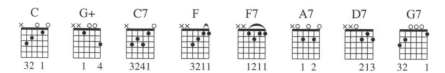

Strum Pattern: 8
Pick Pattern: 8

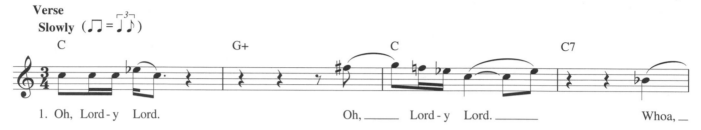

1. Oh, Lord-y Lord. Oh, _____ Lord-y Lord. _____ Whoa, _

_____ it hurt me so bad _____ for _____ us to part. _____ Oh, _____

_____ but some-day, _ ba - by, I ain't gon-na wor'y _____ my life _____

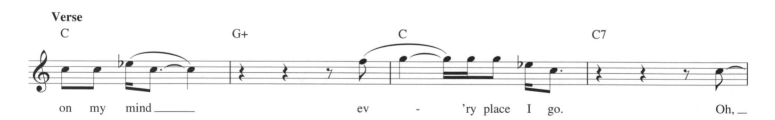

_ an - y - more. _____ 2. You're

Verse

on my mind _____ ev - 'ry place I go. Oh, _

_____ how _ much I love you, ba - by, you will nev - er know.

Copyright © 1941, 1947 SONGS OF UNIVERSAL, INC.
Copyright Renewed
All Rights Reserved   Used by Permission

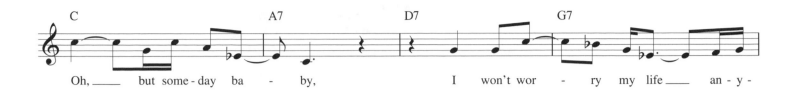
Oh, _____ but some-day ba - by, I won't wor - ry my life_____ an - y -

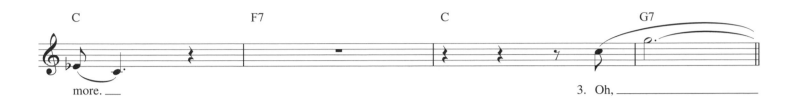
more. _____ 3. Oh, _____

Verse

_____ that's my sto - ry, all _____ I've got to say to you.

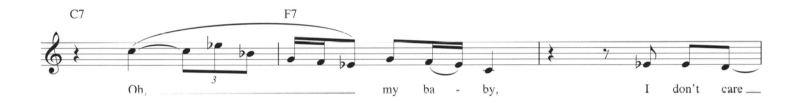
Oh, _____ my ba - by, I don't care_____

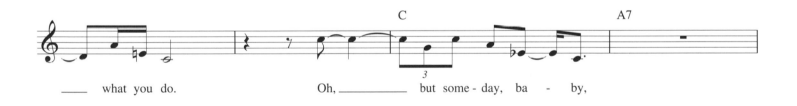
_____ what you do. Oh, _____ but some-day, ba - by,

I ain't gon-na wor - ry my life an - y - more. _____

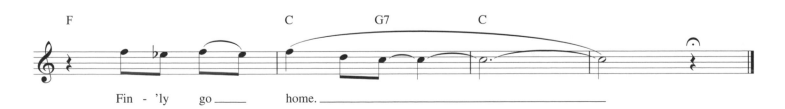
Fin - 'ly go _____ home. _____

Yer Blues

Words and Music by John Lennon and Paul McCartney

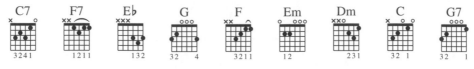

*Strum Pattern: 7, 8
*Pick Pattern: 8, 9

Chorus
Moderate Jazz Waltz

Yes, I'm lone - ly, }
morn - ing, }
wan - na die. ____

*Use Pattern 2 for 4/4 measures

{Yes, I'm lone - ly, }
{In the eve - ning, }

wan - na die. ____
If I

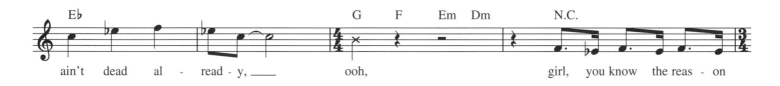

ain't dead al - read - y, ____ ooh, girl, you know the reas - on

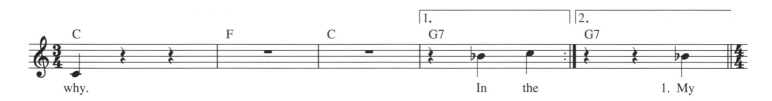

why.
1. In the
2. G7
1. My

Verse
Moderate Rock (♩. = ♩)

mo - ther was of the sky. My fa - ther was of the earth. But
2. *See Additional Lyrics*

I am of the u - ni - verse ___ and you know what it's worth. ____ I'm

Copyright © 1968 Sony/ATV Music Publishing LLC
Copyright Renewed
All Rights Administered by Sony/ATV Music Publishing LLC, 8 Music Square West, Nashville, TN 37203
International Copyright Secured   All Rights Reserved

Additional Lyrics

2. The eagle picks my eye.
   The worm, he licks my bones.
   I feel so suicidal,
   Just like Dylan's Mister Jones.

You Shook Me

Words and Music by Willie Dixon and J.B. Lenoir

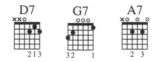

Strum Pattern: 9
Pick Pattern: 9

Verse

Moderately

1. You know you shook me, ba — by.
2. *See Additional Lyrics*

You shook me all ___ night long. ___

You know you shook me, ba — by.

You shook me all ___ night long. _____

Oh, _____

you know you kept on ___ shak-in' me dar - lin,   till you done messed up _____ my _ hap - py home.

1.

2. You know you move

2.

3. Oh, _____

Copyright © 1962 (Renewed 1990) by Arc Music Corporation (BMI) and Hoochie Coochie Music (BMI) /Administered by Bug Music
International Copyright Secured   All Rights Reserved
Used by Permission

Verse

___ some-time _ I won-der   what my poor _ wife and child _ gonna do. ___

Oh, _____ some-time I won-der   what my poor _ wife and child _ gonna do.

Oh, _____ you know you made me mis-treat them, hon-ey.

Oh, _____ I'm mad - ly in love with you.   You know   you

Outro

shook me, ba - by.   You shook me all ___ night _ long. ___

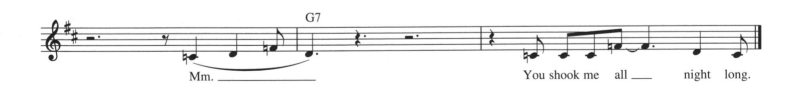

Mm. _____   You shook me all ___ night long.

Additional Lyrics

2. You know you move me baby,
   Just like a hurricane.
   You know you move me baby,
   Just like a hurricane.
   Oh, you know you move me sweetheart,
   Just like an earthquake do the land.

THE BOOK SERIES
FOR EASY GUITAR

THE BEATLES BOOK
An incredible collection of 100 Beatles' favorites, including: And I Love Her • The Ballad of John and Yoko • Birthday • Eleanor Rigby • Good Day Sunshine • Here Comes the Sun • Hey Jude • I Saw Her Standing There • Michelle • Penny Lane • Revolution • Twist and Shout • Yesterday • and more.
00699266 Easy Guitar $19.95

THE BLUES BOOK – 2ND ED.
84 super blues tunes: Baby Please Don't Go • Damn Rigth, I've Got the Blues • Double Trouble • Honest I Do • I'm Your Hoochie Coochie Man • Love Struck Baby • Mean Old World • Milk Cow Blues • Pinetop's Blues • Route 66 • Statesboro Blues • Texas Flood • Trouble in Mind • Who Do You Love • more.
00702104 Easy Guitar $15.95

THE BROADWAY BOOK
93 unforgettable songs from 57 shows! Includes: Ain't Misbehavin' • Beauty and the Beast • Cabaret • Camelot • Don't Cry for Me Argentina • Edelweiss • Hello, Dolly! • I Could Write a Book • Mame • My Favorite Things • One • People • September Song • Some Enchanted Evening • Tomorrow • Try to Remember • Where or When • more.
00702015 Easy Guitar $17.95

THE CHRISTMAS CAROLS BOOK
120 traditional Christmas carols, including: Angels We Have Heard on High • Away in a Manger • Deck the Hall • The First Noel • God Rest Ye Merry, Gentlemen • The Holly and the Ivy • Jingle Bells • Joy to the World • O Holy Night • Silent Night • Still, Still, Still • The Twelve Days of Christmas • We Three Kings of Orient Are • What Child Is This? • and many more.
00702186 Easy Guitar $14.95

THE CHRISTMAS CLASSICS BOOK
100 songs: The Chipmunk Song • Frosty the Snow Man • Grandma Got Run Over by a Reindeer • I'll Be Home for Christmas • Jingle-Bell Rock • Let It Snow! Let It Snow! Let It Snow! • Rudolph the Red-Nosed Reindeer • Silver Bells • We Need a Little Christmas • Wonderful Christmastime • more!
00702200 Easy Guitar $14.95

THE ERIC CLAPTON BOOK
83 favorites from this guitar legend, including: After Midnight • Badge • Bell Bottom Blues • Change the World • Cocaine • I Can't Stand It • I Shot the Sheriff • Lay Down Sally • Layla • Let It Rain • Pretending • Strange Brew • Tears in Heaven • White Room • Wonderful Tonight • more.
00702056 Easy Guitar $18.95

THE CLASSIC COUNTRY BOOK
101 country classics: Act Naturally • Cold, Cold Heart • Could I Have This Dance • Crazy • Daddy Sang Bass • El Paso • Folsom Prison Blues • The Gambler • Heartaches by the Number • I Fall to Pieces • King of the Road • Lucille • Mississippi Woman • Rocky Top • Sixteen Tons • Son-of-a-Preacher Man • Will the Circle Be Unbroken • more.
00702018 Easy Guitar $19.95

Visit Hal Leonard Online at
www.halleonard.com
Prices, contents, and availablilty subject to change without notice.

THE CLASSIC ROCK BOOK
89 huge hits: American Woman • Black Magic Woman • Born to Be Wild • Dust in the Wind • Reelin' in the Years • Revolution • Roxanne • Sweet Home Alabama • Walk This Way • You Really Got Me • and more.
00698977 Easy Guitar $19.95

THE CONTEMPORARY CHRISTIAN BOOK
85 CCM favorites, including: Abba (Father) • Above All • Awesome God • Beautiful • Dive • Friends • His Eyes • How Great Is Our God • Jesus Freak • Lifesong • This Is Your Time • Word of God Speak • and more.
00702195 Easy Guitar $16.95

THE DISNEY SONGS BOOK
73 classic and contemporary Disney favorites, including: Beauty and the Beast • Can You Feel the Love Tonight • It's a Small World • Under the Sea • A Whole New World • You'll Be in My Heart • more.
00702168 Easy Guitar $19.95

THE EARLY ROCK 'N' ROLL BOOK
Over 100 fantastic tunes from rock's early years. Includes: At the Hop • Barbara Ann • Book of Love • Oh, Pretty Woman • Rock Around the Clock • Rockin' Robin • Splish Splash • The Twist • Wooly Bully • and dozens more!
00702179 Easy Guitar $14.95

THE FOLKSONGS BOOK
Over 133 classic folk songs, including: Blow the Man Down • Danny Boy • I've Been Working on the Railroad • Man of Constant Sorrow • Scarborough Fair • Wabash Cannon Ball • When the Saints Go Marching In • Yankee Doodle • more.
00702180 Easy Guitar $14.95

THE GOSPEL SONGS BOOK
Features: Amazing Grace • Blessed Assurance • How Great Thou Art • The Old Rugged Cross • Rock of Ages • Shall We Gather at the River? • Turn Your Radio On • Will the Circle Be Unbroken • and more.
00702157 Easy Guitar $15.95

THE HARD ROCK BOOK
78 hard rock must-haves, including: All Right Now • Bang a Gong (Get It On) • Crazy Train • Hot Blooded • Rock and Roll All Nite • Smells like Teen Spirit • Smoke on the Water • Sweet Child O' Mine • Welcome to the Jungle • and more.
00702181 Easy Guitar $16.95

THE HYMN BOOK
143 glorious hymns: Abide with Me • Amazing Grace • At the Cross • Be Thou My Vision • Blessed Assurance • Fairest Lord Jesus • Holy, Holy, Holy • Just a Closer Walk with Thee • The Old Rugged Cross • Rock of Ages • more.
00702142 Easy Guitar $14.95

THE JAZZ STANDARDS BOOK
100 classics, including: Ain't Misbehavin' • Always • Blue Skies • It Don't Mean a Thing (If It Ain't Got That Swing) • The Lady Is a Tramp • Misty • My Funny Valentine • Slightly Out of Tune (Desafinado) • Stella by Starlight • and more.
00702164 Easy Guitar $15.95

THE LATIN BOOK
102 hot Latin tunes: Amapola • Amor Prohibido • Bésame Mucho • Brazil • Cherry Pink and Apple Blossom White • Cielito Lindo • Granada • Guantanamera • It's Impossible • Mambo No. 5 • Mañana • María Elena • Perfidia • Spanish Eyes • Tango of Roses • Tico Tico • Vaya Con Dios • more.
00702151 Easy Guitar $17.95

THE LOVE SONGS BOOK
100 top love songs: Always • Body and Soul • Cheek to Cheek • Cherish • Don't Know Much • Endless Love • Feelings • Fly Me to the Moon • For All We Know • How Deep Is Your Love • La Vie En Rose • Love Me Tender • Misty • My Romance • Something • You Were Meant for Me • Your Song • more.
00702064 Easy Guitar $16.95

THE NEW COUNTRY HITS BOOK
100 hits by today's top artists! Includes: Achy Breaky Heart • Ain't Going Down ('Til the Sun Comes Up) • Blame It on Your Heart • Boot Scootin' Boogie • Chattahoochee • Down at the Twist and Shout • Friends in Low Places • Neon Moon • Somewhere in My Broken Heart • Small Town Saturday Night • T-R-O-U-B-L-E • The Whiskey Ain't Workin' • more.
00702017 Easy Guitar $19.95

THE ELVIS BOOK
100 songs from The King's career, including: All Shook Up • Are You Lonesome Tonight? • Blue Suede Shoes • Burning Love • Can't Help Falling in Love • Don't Be Cruel (To a Heart That's True) • Heartbreak Hotel • Hound Dog • It's Now or Never • Jailhouse Rock • Love Me Tender • Return to Sender • (Let Me Be Your) Teddy Bear • Viva Las Vegas • and more.
00702163 Easy Guitar $19.95

THE R&B BOOK
Easy arrangements of 89 great hits: ABC • Baby I Need Your Lovin' • Baby Love • Cloud Nine • Dancing in the Street • Easy • I Heard It Through the Grapevine • I'll Be There • I'm So Excited • Man in the Mirror • My Girl • Ooo Baby Baby • Please Mr. Postman • Sexual Healing • Stand by Me • Three Times a Lady • What's Going On • more.
0702058 Easy Guitar $16.95

THE ROCK CLASSICS BOOK
89 rock favorites: Back in the Saddle • Bennie and the Jets • Day Tripper • Evil Ways • For Your Love • Free Ride • Hey Joe • Juke Box Hero • Killer Queen • Low Rider • Oh, Pretty Woman • Pride and Joy • Ramblin' Man • Rhiannon • Smoke on the Water • Young Americans • more.
00702055 Easy Guitar $18.95

THE WEDDING SONGS BOOK
94 songs of love and devotion, including: Always • Endless Love • Grow Old with Me • I Will Be Here • Just the Way You Are • Longer • My Romance • Ode to Joy • This Very Day • Valentine • Wedding March • When You Say Nothing at All • A Whole New World • and many more!
00702167 Easy Guitar $16.95

FOR MORE INFORMATION, SEE YOUR LOCAL MUSIC DEALER, OR WRITE TO:

HAL•LEONARD®
CORPORATION
7777 W. BLUEMOUND RD. P.O. BOX 13819 MILWAUKEE, WI 53213

0408

HAL·LEONARD® EASY RHYTHM GUITAR

EASY RHYTHM GUITAR SERIES

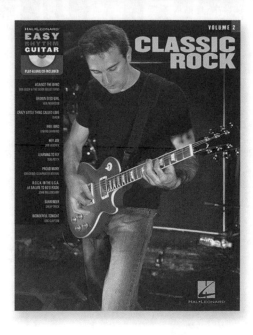

The songs in the **HAL LEONARD EASY RHYTHM GUITAR** books are presented with large, easy-to-read "Rhythm Tab" notation. The rhythm guitar part, or accompaniment, is carefully arranged for beginning to intermediate players. Chord frames are provided to help the player with left-hand fingerings. Lyrics and a melody cue are also included. Just listen to the CD to hear how the guitar should sound, and then play along using the separate backing tracks. The CD is also enhanced so you can use your computer to adjust the recording to any tempo, without changing pitch!

VOL.1 FOLK POP
10 songs: Blowin' in the Wind • Cotton Fields (The Cotton Song) • If I Were a Carpenter • Leaving on a Jet Plane • Lemon Tree • Puff the Magic Dragon • San Francisco (Be Sure to Wear Some Flowers in Your Hair) • This Land Is Your Land • Those Were the Days • Where Have All the Flowers Gone?
00699889 . . . .$14.95

VOL. 2 CLASSIC ROCK
10 songs: Against the Wind • Brown Eyed Girl • Crazy Little Thing Called Love • Free Bird • Hey Joe • Learning to Fly • Proud Mary • R.O.C.K. in the U.S.A. (A Salute to '60s Rock) • Surrender • Wonderful Tonight.
00699898 . . . .$14.95

VOL. 3 '60s POP
10 songs: (It's A) Beautiful Morning • California Dreamin' • Daydream • Happy Together • Hello Mary Lou • I'm a Believer • Let's Get Together • (Sittin' On) The Dock of the Bay • Stand by Me • Walk Away Renee.
00699890 . . . .$14.95

VOL. 4 ACOUSTIC ROCK
10 songs: Band on the Run • Best of My Love • Free Fallin' • Give a Little Bit • Have You Ever Seen the Rain? • Maggie May • Night Moves • Show Me the Way • Teach Your Children • Time for Me to Fly.
00699899 . . . .$14.95

VOL. 5 LATIN
10 songs: A Day in the Life of a Fool (Manha de Carnaval) • Desafinado (Off Key) • The Gift! (Recado Bossa Nova) • The Girl from Ipanema (Garota de Ipanema) • How Insensitive (Insensatez) • Little Boat • More (Ti Guarderò Nel Cuore) • Quizás, Quizás, Quizás (Perhaps, Perhaps, Perhaps) • So Nice (Summer Samba) • Sway (Quien Sera).
00699893 . . . .$14.95

VOL. 6 POP ROCK
10 songs: American Pie • Baby, I Love Your Way • Daniel • Doctor, My Eyes • Don't Stop • Drift Away • Hello, It's Me • If You Leave Me Now • It's Too Late • Summer Breeze.
00699903 . . . .$14.95

FOR MORE INFORMATION,
SEE YOUR LOCAL MUSIC DEALER,
OR WRITE TO:

HAL·LEONARD®
CORPORATION
7777 W. BLUEMOUND RD. P.O. BOX 13819
MILWAUKEE, WISCONSIN 53213

VOL. 7 COUNTRY POP
10 songs: Blue Bayou • Can't Help Falling in Love • The Gambler • Gentle on My Mind • Green Green Grass of Home • (Hey, Won't You Play) Another Somebody Done Somebody Wrong Song • I Can't Stop Loving You • (I Never Promised You A) Rose Garden • King of the Road • Release Me.
00699892 . . . .$14.95

VOL. 8 POP BALLADS
10 songs: Blue Velvet • Crimson and Clover • The End of the World • Greenfields • I Love How You Love Me • In My Room • Let It Be Me (Je T'appartiens) • There's a Kind of Hush (All Over the World) • Walk on By • What the World Needs Now Is Love.
00699894 . . . .$14.95

VOL. 9 MODERN ROCK
10 songs: Clocks • Disarm • Drive • Here Without You • Mr. Jones • Only Wanna Be with You • Push • This Love • Til I Hear It from You • What I Got.
00699905 . . . .$14.95

VOL. 10 FOLK SONGS
10 songs: Beautiful Brown Eyes • Careless Love • (Oh, My Darling) Clementine • Home on the Range • In the Good Old Summertime • Midnight Special • Oh! Susanna • The Red River Valley • Tom Dooley • Will the Circle Be Unbroken.
00699891 . . . .$14.95

Prices, contents, and availability subject to change without notice.

Get Better at Guitar

...with these Great Guitar Instruction Books from Hal Leonard!

101 GUITAR TIPS
INCLUDES TAB

STUFF ALL THE PROS KNOW AND USE
by Adam St. James

This book contains invaluable guidance on everything from scales and music theory to truss rod adjustments, proper recording studio set-ups, and much more. The book also features snippets of advice from some of the most celebrated guitarists and producers in the music business, including B.B. King, Steve Vai, Joe Satriani, Warren Haynes, Laurence Juber, Pete Anderson, Tom Dowd and others, culled from the author's hundreds of interviews.

00695737 Book/CD Pack..........................$16.95

AMAZING PHRASING
INCLUDES TAB

50 WAYS TO IMPROVE YOUR IMPROVISATIONAL SKILLS
by Tom Kolb

This book/CD pack explores all the main components necessary for crafting well-balanced rhythmic and melodic phrases. It also explains how these phrases are put together to form cohesive solos. Many styles are covered – rock, blues, jazz, fusion, country, Latin, funk and more – and all of the concepts are backed up with musical examples. The companion CD contains 89 demos for listening, and most tracks feature full-band backing.

00695583 Book/CD Pack..........................$19.95

BLUES YOU CAN USE
INCLUDES TAB

by John Ganapes

A comprehensive source designed to help guitarists develop both lead and rhythm guitar playing. Covers: Texas, Delta, R&B, early rock and roll, gospel, blues/rock and more. Includes: 21 complete solos • chord progressions and riffs • turnarounds • moveable scales and more. CD features leads and full band backing.

00695007 Book/CD Pack..........................$19.95

FRETBOARD MASTERY
INCLUDES TAB

by Troy Stetina

Untangle the mysterious regions of the guitar fretboard and unlock your potential. *Fretboard Mastery* familiarizes you with all the shapes you need to know by applying them in real musical examples, thereby reinforcing and reaffirming your newfound knowledge. The result is a much higher level of comprehension and retention.

00695331 Book/CD Pack..........................$19.95

FRETBOARD ROADMAPS – 2ND EDITION

ESSENTIAL GUITAR PATTERNS THAT ALL THE PROS KNOW AND USE
by Fred Sokolow

The updated edition of this bestseller features more songs, updated lessons, and a full audio CD! Learn to play lead and rhythm anywhere on the fretboard, in any key; play a variety of lead guitar styles; play chords and progressions anywhere on the fretboard; expand your chord vocabulary; and learn to think musically – the way the pros do.

00695941 Book/CD Pack..........................$14.95

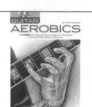

GUITAR AEROBICS
INCLUDES TAB

A 52-WEEK, ONE-LICK-PER-DAY WORKOUT PROGRAM FOR DEVELOPING, IMPROVING & MAINTAINING GUITAR TECHNIQUE
by Troy Nelson

From the former editor of *Guitar One* magazine, here is a daily dose of vitamins to keep your chops fine tuned! Musical styles include rock, blues, jazz, metal, country, and funk. Techniques taught include alternate picking, arpeggios, sweep picking, string skipping, legato, string bending, and rhythm guitar. These exercises will increase speed, and improve dexterity and pick- and fret-hand accuracy. The accompanying CD includes all 365 workout licks plus play-along grooves in every style at eight different metronome settings.

00695946 Book/CD Pack..........................$19.95

GUITAR CLUES
INCLUDES TAB

OPERATION PENTATONIC
by Greg Koch

Join renowned guitar master Greg Koch as he clues you in to a wide variety of fun and valuable pentatonic scale applications. Whether you're new to improvising or have been doing it for a while, this book/CD pack will provide loads of delicious licks and tricks that you can use right away, from volume swells and chicken pickin' to intervallic and chordal ideas. The CD includes 65 demo and play-along tracks.

00695827 Book/CD Pack..........................$19.95

INTRODUCTION TO GUITAR TONE & EFFECTS
by David M. Brewster

This book/CD pack teaches the basics of guitar tones and effects, with audio examples on CD. Readers will learn about: overdrive, distortion and fuzz • using equalizers • modulation effects • reverb and delay • multi-effect processors • and more.

00695766 Book/CD Pack..........................$14.95

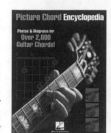

PICTURE CHORD ENCYCLOPEDIA

This comprehensive guitar chord resource for all playing styles and levels features five voicings of 44 chord qualities for all twelve keys – 2,640 chords in all! For each, there is a clearly illustrated chord frame, as well as *an actual photo* of the chord being played! Includes info on basic fingering principles, open chords and barre chords, partial chords and broken-set forms, and more.

00695224 ....$19.95

SCALE CHORD RELATIONSHIPS
INCLUDES TAB

by Michael Mueller & Jeff Schroedl

This book teaches players how to determine which scales to play with which chords, so guitarists will never have to fear chord changes again! This book/CD pack explains how to: recognize keys • analyze chord progressions • use the modes • play over nondiatonic harmony • use harmonic and melodic minor scales • use symmetrical scales such as chromatic, whole-tone and diminished scales • incorporate exotic scales such as Hungarian major and Gypsy minor • and much more!

00695563 Book/CD Pack..........................$14.95

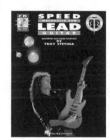

SPEED MECHANICS FOR LEAD GUITAR
INCLUDES TAB

Take your playing to the stratosphere with the most advanced lead book by this proven heavy metal author. *Speed Mechanics* is the ultimate technique book for developing the kind of speed and precision in today's explosive playing styles. Learn the fastest ways to achieve speed and control, secrets to make your practice time really count, and how to open your ears and make your musical ideas more solid and tangible. Packed with over 200 vicious exercises including Troy's scorching version of "Flight of the Bumblebee." Music and examples demonstrated on CD. 89-minute audio.

00699323 Book/CD Pack..........................$19.95

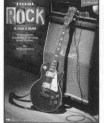

TOTAL ROCK GUITAR
INCLUDES TAB

A COMPLETE GUIDE TO LEARNING ROCK GUITAR
by Troy Stetina

This unique and comprehensive source for learning rock guitar is designed to develop both lead and rhythm playing. It covers: getting a tone that rocks • open chords, power chords and barre chords • riffs, scales and licks • string bending, strumming, palm muting, harmonics and alternate picking • all rock styles • and much more. The examples are in standard notation with chord grids and tab, and the CD includes full-band backing for all 22 songs.

00695246 Book/CD Pack..........................$17.95

FOR MORE INFORMATION, SEE YOUR LOCAL MUSIC DEALER, OR WRITE TO:

HAL•LEONARD® CORPORATION
7777 W. BLUEMOUND RD. P.O. BOX 13819 MILWAUKEE, WI 53213

Visit Hal Leonard Online at
www.halleonard.com

Prices, contents, and availability subject to change without notice.

0308